ONE
BLOKE

Dedication

For Marjorie, whose love and confidence, steadfast support and practical advice underpinned this venture and prevented excess enthusiasm from sinking it.

© Barry Seddon 2011
Published by The Bluecoat Press, Liverpool
Book design by March Design, Liverpool
Printed by www.scandinavianbook.co.uk

ISBN 9781908457028

Thanks to our daughter Helen, whose research filled in the branches of Paul's family tree. The staff who helped us for 20 years at Greater Manchester County Record Office. Simon Henniker, for two painstaking years and his photo-digitising contribution. Marie, Pat, Ken, Vincent, Maureen, Nic, John, Andrew, Brother Industries, Martin, the folk clubs, the singers, the musicians and all the others. They know who they are.

In Memory of David Anthony Hall who was a close friend of Paul Graney for many years. After Paul died and we began to catalogue his priceless archive, it was David who found the Memory Tapes. Together we listened to them. They told the story of One Bloke ... the book in your hands. He longed to see it in print and although his sad death last Christmas meant that could never be, he always knew that he was the one who struck the spark. Thank-you, David. Go well.

ONE
BLOKE

A Manchester man's
tale of two decades

Paul Graney
Edited by Barry Seddon

THE BLUECOAT PRESS

CONTENTS

Preface by Ruth and Edmund Frow 6

Introduction by Barry Seddon 8

Behind the Bloke Paul's family tree 12

EARLY DAYS

Chapter 1 Hard Knocks 16

Chapter 2 Boggarts 25

THE BRITISH WORKING MAN

Chapter 3 Iron and Brass 34

Chapter 4 Strike! 46

Chapter 5 Tricks and No Trade 57

Chapter 6 Dole Days 64

ON THE ROAD

Chapter 7 Fifty Thousand Dossers 75

Chapter 8 The Spike 83

Chapter 9 Tales over the Table 89

Chapter 10 Conger and Tinwhistle 98

Chapter 11 Tents and Old Timers 103

Chapter 12 Tales of My Own 108

Chapter 13 One Thousand Days of Nothing 115

Chapter 14 The Visible Poor 122

THE SHIRTLESS THIRTIES

Chapter 15 Food for Thought 126

Chapter 16 A Penny for 'Em 133

Chapter 17 Kids' Stuff 138

MARCHING AND FIGHTING

Chapter 18 Wet Blankets　… … … … … … … … … 149

Chapter 19 Sore Feet　… … … … … … … … … … 157

Chapter 20 Black Shirts and Bludgeons　… … … … 162

CROSS-CHANNEL

Chapter 21 Dutch Treats　… … … … … … … … … 175

Chapter 22 German Lessons　… … … … … … … … 183

Chapter 23 Vienna to Munich　… … … … … … … 191

TIME OUT

Chapter 24 That Sporting Life　… … … … … … … 196

Chapter 25 Tenting Tonight　… … … … … … … … 209

Chapter 26 Mad Lem Wragge　… … … … … … … 216

Chapter 27 Left-Winging　… … … … … … … … … 220

Chapter 28 Curtain Calls　… … … … … … … … … 224

Chapter 29 Back to Reality　… … … … … … … … 230

Remembering Paul　… … … … … … … … … … 235

They talked to Paul　… … … … … … … … … … 241

Afterword　… … … … … … … … … … … … … 258

Glossary　… … … … … … … … … … … … … 262

Old money to new　… … … … … … … … … … 271

PREFACE

A charcoal sketch made at Harry Boardman's house.

Written in 1994 by Labour activists Edmund and Ruth Frow, founders of the Working Class Movement Library, Salford.

Paul Graney's account of his life during the inter-war years is a lively and fascinating read. He was a many-sided individualist, with a social conscience and an appealing way of landing himself in hot water. He was not an intellectual (a point which he emphasises) but he was self-educated in the important aspects of life and he participated in spheres of activity beyond the limits of the majority of lads brought up in the slums of Manchester.

Raised in North East Lancashire, he was always proud of being a Lancashire lad and traced his athletic ability to his early years on the moors around Nelson. He excelled in walking, boxing, and other physical activities, which stood him in good stead when he found himself in rough company among tramps and dossers and when he met Fascist thugs on the Continent.

He took part in the Workers Theatre Movement with Ewan MacColl and Joan Littlewood. He was a rambler, and campaigned for access to the mountains. He was a member of the Workers' Arts Club at Hyndman Hall in Salford, where he met Walter Greenwood and joined fellow left-wingers in their activities.

As an unemployed youth, he joined the National Unemployed Workers' Movement and took part in Hunger Marches and demonstrations. He was present in Manchester on 8 October 1931, when fire hoses were turned on the marchers. He was in the North West contingent which joined the Jarrow marchers on their way to London.

The Youth Hostel Association also benefited from his considerable organising activity and energy.

As a raconteur, he had few equals. His memory remained clear throughout his long life and Barry Seddon has performed a near miracle in reducing to manageable proportions the more than 100,000 words of reminiscence, which Paul dictated on to 16 hours of tape cassettes.

Throughout his life, Paul Graney collected songs and social history recordings. *One Bloke* is a compelling read for young people who want to know what life was really like in the good/bad old days, for the not so young who remember them and for anyone who has time to spare to settle down to enjoy a good yarn.

INTRODUCTION

WHEN Paul Graney, the premier North West folklorist, was 65, not long since made redundant by the CWS from his job as a pipe fitter, I was a brash stripling of 35, in my first year as the *Manchester Evening News's* first Folk Music Columnist. The capitals reflect how important I thought the job was. One night, Paul was pointed out to me at a folk concert in a church hall near Manchester Grammar School. This was the man whose name I had seen in 'song-found-by' tributes, on records by folk music legends such as Martin Carthy, Dave Burland, Vin Garbutt and the Watersons. Maybe he would talk to me for the column? I blush at the memory! Lacking a formal introduction, I breezed up to the burly chap in the well-worn sports jacket. "Excuse me please? Are you Paul Graney?"

He turned from the tape recorder with which he had been tinkering. Pale blue eyes gazed at me. "Aye, that's right."

"My name's Barry Seddon. I write the folk column for the *Evening News*."

"Hmm! Well, don't let it get you down, lad!"

I suppose my laughing reaction must have suited Paul, because over the next nine years, until his death in June 1982, two months short of his 74th birthday, I was pleased to be one of those he called a friend. We even opened our own off-beat folk club, at the Ring o' Bells, Middleton, where the crack was as important as the music and an evening with no songs at all was not unusual.

Paul never learned to drive; his considerable travelling was all by public transport or on foot. In his later years, I was one of many who ferried him to and from folk clubs to see artists, famous and otherwise, who matched up to his well-developed sense of what constituted folk music.

But folk music and folklore were only part of this irreverent, kind-hearted (and sometimes downright cussed) man's fascinating life. At least once a week, back from some folk club or other, we would sit in my old car outside his one-room flat at 4 Carlton Road, Whalley Range, Manchester. As prostitutes walked their beats in nearby Withington Road, Paul would talk about his life and the lives of those whose paths he had crossed.

Breathing in his distinctive aroma of Brylcream and pipe smoke, I realised that these sad, funny, whimsical or tragic stories were treasures too important and well-observed to be lost, but when I said so, he seemed honestly embarrassed and I eventually stopped asking him to let me interview him. But Paul did not forget. When he died in hospital, he left in my care his enormous collection of tape recordings: 300 reels and almost 500 cassettes. Among the cassettes were 16 mysterious ones labelled M1 to M16. 'M' stood for memory.

In the unembarrassing seclusion of his flat, just two years before he died, Paul had dictated the story of his life, almost to the start of World War Two, with emphasis on the momentous years between the First World War and the Second. Now Paul's 105,000 words have become 65,000 – the story which is now this book.

Meanwhile, with much help from a long-standing friend of Paul's, Manchester folk musician David Hall, the Paul Graney Memorial Folk Trust was established. Its prime aim was to raise cash to save Paul's treasure trove of tapes. They were mostly of poor quality, because he could never afford the best. Many were dangerously brittle, from being stored in a cupboard beside a gas fire.

The task of transferring their irreplaceable contents on to high quality archive discs took more than 20 years, in a small rent-free room at the Greater Manchester County Record Office. Many contents lists were missing, but fortunately, David had an eidetic memory and used it to great effect. Simon Henniker was a valuable recruit for the final years, a Heritage Lottery grant paying his wages.

The Record Office job completed, we passed the now-computerised collection into the care of former folk singer John Adams, who ran the tradition-based Village Media Project at Salford University. The original recordings and the DVD version are in the care of Andrew Schofield, who manages the North West Sound Archive at Clitheroe Castle – not far from Paul's boyhood town of Nelson.

Paul's archive is a unique magpie mixture ... songs by well-known folk singers when they were absolute beginners; street festivals and children's game-songs; Maori chants picked up on shortwave radio; backward bagpipe music (Paul twisted the tape when loading it in a hurry); and above all, the interviews ...

As later extracts demonstrate, Paul was fascinated by people and their stories. One of his most moving recordings is of Mrs Anderton, an elderly Salford woman, remembering her time in the workhouse, nearly a century before.

The man who recorded this and other interviews had a fascinating life of his own. His Memory Tapes tell of: the Depression, when he and thousands of others took to the roads, to find work; the General Strike, in which Paul was a vigorous union activist; Oswald Mosley and his Blackshirts – Paul was injured by Fascists on two occasions; The Hunger Marches – Paul trained and accompanied the Manchester contingent to London; the rise of the Nazis – Paul witnessed one of Hitler's hysterical rallies and Hitler Youth members burning books in Berlin.

Paul also played a backstage role in the Manchester and Salford theatrical scenes, with Joan Littlewood and Jimmy Miller (who later became folk singer Ewan MacColl).

He helped to set up the Youth Hostels Association and was present at early Mass Trespasses, which opened up the mountains and moorlands of Derbyshire.

Paul Graney, an ordinary Lancashire lad who would come home from school in Nelson and run up and down Pendle Hill before teatime, turned into an extraordinary man, his life shaped by traumatic times.

The book you now hold is the end result of the Trust's other main aim – to bring Paul Graney's story to as many people as possible.

Paul never claimed to be anything more than 'just one bloke'. This book came from his head, and from his heart.

Barry Seddon

Paul Graney, the famous pipe was rarely far away.

BEHIND THE BLOKE

FOR many people, Paul Graney's death left unanswered questions, particularly about his roots. All I knew was where he was born and that he had a mother, sister, father and step-father. Who were the other people on the branches of his family tree? And how did a Manchester born boy end up in Nelson?

Paul hints in Chapter 24 and elsewhere that he had seen Second World War army service, but I have not been able to track down any records of this. Likewise, although he talks (in Chapter 22) about having a look at Spain in 1934, stories that he fought in the Spanish Civil War between 1936 and 1939 as a member of the anti-Franco International Brigade, remain unconfirmed.

However, the outstanding puzzles have now been solved, thanks to sensible suggestions by my 'practical detective' wife Marjorie, and to thorough research by our librarian daughter Helen.

Paul's grandfather was Michael Graney. He was born and married in Ireland. He and Paul's grandmother, the former Ellen Kelly, had ten sons between 1851 and 1872. The first was born in Warrington, the next eight in Flint, North Wales, and the last in Farnworth, near Bolton, after the family moved there. Ellen died in 1891.

Paul's father, Joseph Graney, was the sixth son, born in 1863. He had five children with his wife Elizabeth Cummings, whose parents and siblings had moved to Scotland from Wales before the 1891 Census.

Shortly after 1891, Joseph and Elizabeth and their family must have joined them because their fourth and fifth children were born in Scotland in 1893 and 1898.The family stayed in Scotland, appearing on the 1901 and 1911 Scotland Censuses, but Joseph is not there with them; he appears instead in Manchester, where he had joined some of his brothers.

Paul's mother was Eleanor Ryder, who preferred to be called Nellie. She was born in Hulme, Manchester, in 1876. By the 1891 Census, she was living with William, her 49 year-old widower father, her sister and her four brothers, in Derby Street, Hulme. She was 15 and working as a domestic servant. At the age of 23, on 18 April 1900, and living in Weaste, Salford, she married Roger Taylor, a 26 year-old clerk from Kearsley, near Farnworth, at nearby St Luke's church. Their daughter Sarah Florence was born in 1901. Roger died in 1907 aged 33.

Paul's father, Joseph Graney, by this time employed in the steel industry, must have come on to the scene not long afterwards and befriended the new widow. On 3 August 1908, little more than a year after Roger Taylor's death, Paul was born at 16 James Street, Bradford, Manchester. On his birth certificate, his mother's name appears as 'Nellie Graney, previously Taylor, formerly Ryder' with Joseph Graney named as his father. However, despite diligent searches, no record could be found of Nellie and Joseph Graney marrying.

What happened to Joseph after this time is uncertain. One possibility is that his wife and family went to America and he rejoined them there.

Nellie's move to Nelson seems to have come after a period in Rochdale. The 1911 Census shows her living there with Paul (aged 2) and his half-sister Sarah Florence (10), at the home of Nellie's youngest brother, Arthur Ryder. He worked as a canal boatman and was married with three children. Three adults and five children in a two-roomed house! A move to Nelson must have seemed very attractive to Nellie.

Paul's stepfather was William Thomas Sewell, a 27 year-old quarry worker from Rochdale. In June 1911, Nellie married him in Rochdale, describing herself as 'Nellie Taylor, widow'.

If all this seems eventful, consider Paul's own story. His opening scene is the brooding slopes of Pendle Hill, rearing over Nelson from the Lancashire plain, like a whale rising from the waves. Here, as a young boy, during the excitement of a bonfire, he learned an early lesson – that pleasure often leads to pain.

EARLY DAYS

CHAPTER 1

HARD KNOCKS

IT WAS 1919 ... my last full year at school. I was eleven. The war had been over for twelve months and it had left me partially blinded. Celebrations on the first anniversary of Armistice Day had included lighting the chain of old Napoleonic beacons throughout the country. In Nelson, our nearest beacon was on top of Pendle Hill, about two and a half miles away. Fireworks were going off and everybody was going mad and someone threw a firework which exploded very near my right eye.

The nearest hospital, in Barrowford, was full of soldiers, so it was a doctor job. There was no Panel then, the early name for the National Health Service. If you went to the doctor, you had to pay. I finished up with bandages round my eye for about a month, then a black eye shade that made me look a bit like Long John Silver, then dark glasses for nearly twelve months. There's still a burn mark on my right eye. So yes, indirectly I was a war casualty.

At the age of twelve in the mill towns you went half-timing – morning to school and afternoons to the mill, and the following week reversed. Nine-tenths of the kids, both lads and girls, went with their parents, who worked in the mill. I had a job called minding, or tenting. You weren't supposed to do a lot, just help. But, of course, like most jobs that start out being nice, it didn't finish nice

Thirsty (photograph Paul Graney).

and I usually ended up doing most of the hard and dirty work. I went with my mother and my sister, so it wasn't too bad during the half-timing period. They had four looms each, made up of four plains or twills, two dobbies or patterns, and two check looms with ballow ends.

Between us, we had to mind these old Lancashire looms. Someone had to be with them all the time. If you had a 'tenter', you could safely go for your own weft, or go to the toilet. But if you left them running unattended, the shuttle could run out and then the loom would stop, or one of the threads would break. This was what they

17

called 'an end down'. It would tangle itself up and you would find yourself with a couple of hours' work scratching out the mark that it had made in the cloth, pulling all the threads back. If not, you would get that piece of cloth back at the end of the week. When it went upstairs to the cutlooker, or the clothlooker, he would cut out about a couple of yards each side of it, wrap it up, and you would receive it with your wages with the appropriate value deducted. So you were very careful about spoiling the cloth and avoided getting thick parts in the weft. You had to watch it all the time.

Part of my job was to fetch up the weft every other day. It was kept in skips in a dark, gas-lit cellar. You loaded up a big tin box and carried it back on your shoulder – heavy work for a young lad. Then you carried the cuts out, when the mark came up on the warp. It was cut across and folded and you took it into the warehouse with a tag on it to show who'd woven it.

You got used to a fair amount of work, but it was the monotony and noise as much as anything that wore you down and also the discipline of constantly having to be there, watching all the time for anything going wrong in the cloth and stopping the loom.

The big weaving sheds had thick walls and were sky-lit via window channels in the roof, which made them very hot in summer and very cold in winter. Everything had a coating of lint, a fine throwing off of fibres from the cloth, which used to gather about an inch thick underneath the looms every day and you had to sweep it out. It was always floating around in the air and it used to choke you, but you couldn't get a drink of water. You weren't allowed to take a can of water in with you and the only water available was locked in the brewing place behind a wire fence, to be unlocked only at meal times. You started work at 6am and your first half-hour break was at 8.15am; at dinnertime you got three quarters of an hour. We were lucky that we lived right across the road from the mill and it was as quick to run home as it was to line up for the hot water at the mill. Those who stayed were not allowed to have their meal inside the mill, so when they'd brewed they often sat in the weft cellar. It was frowned on, but it wasn't always stopped. If it was fine, they would go out into the mill yard, turn a skip bottom-up and sit on that.

One thing about working in the mill sticks vividly in my mind. It was common, almost universal, to initiate new lads. There were a few male weavers, but most were women and they were the ones that did it. When they decided you had settled down after a couple of weeks, one or two of them would follow you to the weft cellar and three or four more would follow them. They would crowd round you in a dark spot, pull your pants down and rub you with thick, dirty grease which had been cleaned off the looms; on top of that they'd pile all the lint from the sweepings – a sort of tarring and feathering. Very unpleasant, especially for a young lad. It certainly stuck in my mind. When I cried out they put a bag over my face, so I couldn't be heard.

From then on, every time I passed these girls they'd start sniggering and I was consumed with plans for revenge. I never achieved it, but I used to look at them and think: "Well, so you're one of them … you'll pay for it!" That gave me a certain satisfaction, and I think it saved me from getting a hang-up about it. I've known lads who wouldn't go into the mills because they knew what went on, but for most there was very little work in

Nelson outside the mills.

When I was still full-time at school I used to get a Saturday penny and sometimes when my mother was a bit flush, she would give me enough for the Saturday morning matinee at the pictures. I think it cost tuppence. But usually I just got a penny to spend on what I liked. My mother would buy me a weekly comic – *Chips, Comic Cuts, Funny Wonder, Butterfly* – I can't remember them all but I would get one, then swap with one of the other kids.

As a half-timer I didn't actually get paid, but my spends went up to threepence and I had to pay for myself at the pictures on a Saturday morning. Actually I could go only on alternate weeks, because the mills were open on Saturday mornings until they stopped the engines at noon. Then you had to clean your looms down in your own time; a good sweeping to remove all the lint. That was my job while my mother went shopping. I would be there with the brush and rags, until all trace of the lint had been removed. But the year after I went full time, they abolished this and practically abolished half-time as well. The law dictated that half-timing would be abolished in 1919, but the mill owners were given a period of grace and it varied from shed to shed. Our shed, Foulds Mill in Morris Street, where I lived, went on with half-time practically into 1921 and other mills went longer than that.

Half-timing was a waste of twelve months' education, because the school didn't want to know you. They couldn't deal with classes that were only there half a day at a time. For about four months before I left school altogether, they sat about a dozen of us in an empty room with some books to read and just left us there, bobbing in now and then to see we weren't getting up to mischief.

Then the school leaving age was raised to thirteen. That was in 1921, but by this time I was already twelve and working full time. I'd left the weaving shed and was 'reaching-in', helping a loomer to get the warp ready for the looms, in a quiet room such as they had in every mill warehouse. The place I worked was Jimmy Nelson's, about a mile and a half across town. There were about 15 loomers, each with his own young reacher-in.

We were not paid by the firm. We were employed by the man we worked with, the loomer. I'll never forget the man I worked with – Ralph Mawhood. He was a drinking friend of my stepfather's, a big drinker as was my stepfather. He got me the job with this chap, who would give my wages to my stepfather. A lad was supposed to be paid a percentage of what the loomer earned, but if he didn't pay you at all you had no redress. Well, I never knew what was going on. This chap used to meet my stepfather in the band club in Nelson and he would pay him over the beer. I think at this time my mother found out I was getting about twelve shillings a week, which was pretty good money for a young lad, but she didn't get any of it, of course, my stepfather being such a drunkard, but she somehow managed to winkle fourpence a week for me out of this twelve shillings.

I couldn't afford to go to the pictures often. Working full-time, I couldn't go to the tuppenny Saturday morning show. There were no Saturday afternoon matinees and at night the cheapest seats were about threepence. But I'd get an occasional penny bag of toffees and a comic now and again.

Reaching in was a job and a half. This is how it worked – the warp beam, with all its reeds [*threads*] hanging down, was set up in a wooden frame and the lad sat behind, holding his own handful of threads. The loomer pushed his little reed hook, with anything up to four hooks on it, through the healds [*eyelets*] in the reeds and the reacher-in lad had to catch his threads on to the hooks – in the right order, mind you, not crossed from the warp.

For the first week, your shoulders ached with lifting your hand up and down. My mother used to rub them with goose grease and horse liniment, but I couldn't lift my hand. And as that wears off, your fingers start to bleed where the threads cut them. It's real agony and there's nothing you can do except wait until they harden, until you get a seg – a piece of hard skin in the crack of your first and second fingers.

It was also quite usual to come home with your legs bleeding. You sat on a little three-legged stool facing the loomer, but with all the reeds and healds in front of you, you couldn't see him; all you saw was his hooks coming through and when they started waving furiously it meant you were going too slowly, you should have been ready to hook on. He wouldn't wait and just shoved the hooks through and back again and you had to be there ready to hook the bits of cotton on to them. If you kept him waiting two or three times, the next thing would be a kick on the shins from his clogs. "Come on! Hurry up! Come on! Come on!" And he'd kick you again and again. I've still got ridges in my shinbones where I was kicked. I came home many a time bleeding and my mother would have to put plasters and ointment on, usually Vaseline. At that time I didn't wear long trousers, they weren't very much in the vogue. I wore thick, long black stockings, clogs, and dark grey knickerbockers with a couple of buttons below the knee. I was about 15 before I got into long trousers, and there were still lads of my age running around in short trousers.

You'd come home and roll your stockings down, and there would be all the bruises and the blood. But nobody said anything. It was all accepted. I remember once when there was snow. We'd been throwing a few snowballs in the mill yard and a mill tackler came round the warehouse, trapped us, then took every lad in turn by the scruff of the neck and gave him a real pasting.

I suppose it was a continuation of the brutality in the schools. You had no rights there, either. The school I was at before I went full-time at the mill, was a primitive sort of place; a former Sunday school rigged up as an elementary. I knew one lad who went there that had his little finger broken by our teacher with the cane. We were in Standard Three and she was a big fat Scotswoman, Miss Crawford. I'll never forget her name, or her face. I'm 70 now and I still have a clear picture of her in my mind. Her face is as familiar to me as Hitler's.

She would walk along behind the desks while we were writing or doing sums. She had a cane that was about two feet six inches long and about half an inch thick. She would creep up behind you, and you wouldn't know because the rule was strict: get your head down and keep it down. So you'd be looking at your piece of paper, your book or whatever, and if she saw something wrong – bang! Hard on the back of your fingers with the cane.

All this was quite normal. I've been strapped many a time in the headmaster's study, when I'd not done anything. There was a bunch of us and when anything happened and they couldn't find the culprit, it was presumed that one of us was responsible.

One thing used to happen though that none of our lot was ever involved in. The lads and girls were segregated in the school yard by a big high wall, but if you climbed on top of the boys' toilets you could look into the girls' toilets, and some boys did this, and the girls saw them. Of course they reported it, we got the blame and it was off to the headmaster and bend over for the strap. He used a piece of belting out of the mill, which was even worse than the cane.

But you accepted it. You felt the injustice, but you never thought about it as brutality, it was just something that you lived with.

CHAPTER 2

BOGGARTS

Nelson, where it all began. Pendle Hill is in the background.

EVEN BEFORE I started half-timing, my childhood was distinctly lacking in halcyon days. We were beset by monsters at every turn. We weren't safe indoors and outside, there were witches, boggarts, everything, lying in wait. In the gentler South of England, they had fairies, elves and gnomes. But not in the rough old North, where there were monsters hidden amongst the flowers, even in the streams, just waiting to get you.

Living beside Pendle Hill, naturally witches entered into a lot of our activities, merely a skip and a jump from the homes of the famous Pendle Witches. Alice Nutter had lived at Roughlee, about half an hour's walk away, and we'd amble around Roughlee Hall, which is now in ruins, and an old ruined house in the woods towards Newchurch, which we always thought was Mother Demdyke's place.

Any old woman, if she had a limp, wore odd clothes, dribbled a bit, or was different in any way at all, was automatically a witch. We were too frightened to shout or chase them and if we saw one coming, wearing a long black skirt and a black shawl over her head, we'd cross the road and for the rest of our journey wouldn't tread on any cracks in the pavement. It's well-known that the Devil waits under the flagstones and if anyone puts both feet on a crack, he will open it and drag him down to Hell. Everybody knows that.

Some women could work a sort of magic. My mother knew all about herbs, for instance. We always had bunches hanging to dry in our pantry. Nearly every Sunday we'd go out yarding, picking herbs for her. She'd make bottles of this and that for neighbours and their children. Her rubbing bottle could take the pain out of a strain. She would almost certainly once have been classed as a witch.

Our commonest monsters were boggarts. Lancashire and Manchester folklore books are full of them – eye witness accounts, carefully documented and described. Some historians say the word comes from the

Scandinavian bargeest, a bear ghost or spirit of the woods. But you can find a link in the West Indies, where a mischievous spirit manifests itself as a boogerman.

In the Isle of Man the boogan takes the roof off churches which are being built. In Burnley, when the parish church was being built, several hundred years ago, every morning when they came to put the roof on they found the previous day's work scattered. It happened several times despite a watch being kept. Then someone remembered that this was a boggart's playground and the church was rebuilt on the site where it stands today.

I first heard the story of the Barrowford boggart when I was young, but since then I've heard it transposed to many different places, like so many folk tales. The original boggart however, haunted a house in Barrowford, near Nelson. One night a local lad slept there for a bet. Towards midnight he was awakened by the bed shaking and a voice saying, "Now then, lad, there's only thee and me." He put his head under the sheets, determined to stay, and the bed shook even harder. Eventually, after about the fifth time of, "Now then, lad, there's only thee and me", he said, "Now look, boggart, if you'll let me get my boots on, there'll only be thee."

It's only about ten years since the last report of the black rabbit of Rochdale in the parish churchyard. This is an unusual boggart, in that it's like the banshees of Ireland, foretelling death, either of the one who sees it, or one of his family. In the parish register there is an account of a parson seeing this rabbit on the church wall but it doesn't say whether the prophecy of doom came true. But about 1970 the papers were full of someone seeing it again and a member of his family dying.

In Manchester, there are written accounts of women

27

seeing a dog as big as a cow on what is now Didsbury golf course. Every old hall and district of the city has its own boggart. When Deansgate was a narrow street, full of thugs and robbers, a huge headless black dog would chase drunks and knock them down. A priest exorcised it and buried its spirit under a stone at Blackfriars Bridge for 999 years. That was only 120 years ago, so we can still walk with safety on Deansgate.

But the most famous of the Manchester boggarts was the one at Boggart Hole Clough, Blackley. It was a poltergeist and was unusual in that it was heard to speak, though was never seen. The Clough is now a public park, but the boggart was there when it was Bell's Farm. It would milk the cows, drink its fill and throw the rest all over the shippen floor. It would steal an egg for its breakfast, then leave all the others smashed. It would turn milk sour and cut the legs off chairs and tables. Oh, it was an evil little thing. It lived in the kitchen, behind a board with a hole in it. If you put your finger through, it would catch hold of it and not let go for days. Its victim would have to be fed where he stood.

Farmer Bell decided to flit to another farm. He secretly gathered all his stuff together, loaded it on a cart and set off down the dell to the main road. On the way he said to his wife, "I'm glad we're shut of that boggart." From one of the milk churns came a voice, "Eh, you haven't got rid of me. I'm flitting with thee." The farmer threw up his hands in despair, turned around and went back home. That's the legend, and there's a song about it, too.

Of course, boggarts were often a device used to keep children out of danger and this could have been one of them, because Buckley Hall once stood at the top of Buckley Hall Clough and in it was a large and dangerous pond, so it's highly likely that parents renamed the place to frighten the kids away. A similar tale was told at Gisburn, about Skrikin' Annie, who caught young children, took them to her kitchen, skinned them, and hung up their skins to dry – a legend calculated to stop any kid from going up on the moor!

One of the most terrifying tales of my childhood was that of Jenny Greenteeth, a water witch who lived under the green slime of stagnant ponds. A child, seeing such a pond, could very easily be kidded into thinking it was solid and find himself under water. My mother would say, "You've not been near that water, have you?" I'd reply, "No" and she'd say, "Think on you don't, with Jenny Greenteeth under there waiting to get you. She'll have somebody yet, and it might be you."

At the bottom of the hill, five minutes from where I lived, was a park with a stream, Pendle Waters. There were big deep pools in this stream, where one or two kids had actually drowned. So we were warned not to go near, this time because of the bloodsuckers. They were leeches, of course, but we called them 'snigs', and firmly believed what we'd been told, that if you got one on you, it would suck out all the blood and leave just a skeleton with a bit of skin round it. If we were near that stream for any purpose, and kids always had some reason to go near it, we would first search for snigs, by turning stones over with a stick. And if we found any, we wouldn't go near the water. And of course there were plenty of them, so our parents' warnings worked.

Even the wild flowers held menace. There was a tiny white one that grew in the hedges. I never knew its name, but we called it Mother Prick My Eyes Out. We believed that if you waved it about in front of your eyes you would go blind. Then we had madweed, which I've since found out is ragwort. It is one of about half a dozen plants classified by the Ministry of Agriculture as noxious weeds. If you grow them in the garden they will tell you to get rid of them and if you don't they will prosecute you, because ragwort, along with one or two others, has hallucinatory properties.

The foxglove was another we were warned to keep clear of. It was known as Marrow Melter, because if you ate its flowers or leaves it would melt the marrow in your bones and you would fall down like a bag of jelly wrapped in skin. A horrifying thought. We were not taught to be afraid of dying. Dying for a child is incomprehensible, but you can understand your bones turning to jelly, going mad, having all the blood sucked out of you, or a boggart skinning you.

I was sometimes terrified to go out, but even in the house, dangers lurked. I would run in to get a drink of water, couldn't be bothered with a cup, so I'd just stick my head under the tap and drink that way. My grandmother, who lived with us then, would play blue murder if she saw me. Didn't I know that a water wolf lurked behind every tap? This was a sort of furry beetle which got down your throat, fastened itself to your stomach and ate all your food until you starved to death. Eventually her warnings took effect; I'm 72 now, and when I get a glass of water from the tap I always throw the first one away and look carefully at the second before drinking. It's habit. It was knocked into me.

At the bottom of our street in Nelson ran the Leeds and Liverpool canal. Apparently I fell into it when I was about three, at Barrowford. It was a serious do – off to hospital to be pumped out, but I don't remember, and it didn't seem to have had any restraining effect on me. I was forever along the bank, which was a treasure-trove of planks, lumps of interesting wood, empty cans and dead roach and perch. One thing we'd do was find one or two dead fish and hide them in a dry stone wall. Soon they would be full of maggots which we scooped into an old tin to sell to a fisherman for a penny. If our parents had known about our maggot farm they would have killed us.

One of the canal warnings we were given was to beware of giant water rats, which would drag us under. Well, we'd seen rats, quite big ones too, but no giants. Until one day I saw a thing about 30 inches long, swimming across the canal towards me. I ran for my life and when I looked back it was on the bank, heading off across the moor. I didn't realise until years later that it must have been an otter. It was a long time before I ever ventured on the canal bank again and I never went up to that particular area.

I've already mentioned our school teacher, Miss Crawford. We always swore she was a witch because she did some very surprising things. We never saw her arrive or leave the school. Everybody wondered about her. And naturally she got tagged as a witch. She was well past middle age, a Scot – we often got the cane because we couldn't understand what she said, but she could read our minds! One time I remember vividly, word had got around that if you put a piece of horsehair on the palm of your hand when you were about to have the cane, it wouldn't hurt. Horsehair was easily obtainable because most traffic was horse-drawn, so I got two or three lengths of it. We'd discussed it in the playground, me and my two cronies and decided to try it next time we got the cane. But no sooner were we back in school than she said:

"Graney! Come out here!" Puzzled, I went out to the front. "Would you like to try it now?"

"What, Miss?"

"Your piece of horsehair. Would you like to give it a try? Just put a piece on your hand and hold your hand out?"

Bang! Oooh! It didn't work. I never figured out how she knew. My mates hadn't said anything. They hadn't had time. We'd gone straight in from the playground to the classroom and she'd called me out straight away. We even thought she might have seen us from the classroom window, until we realised it was too high. We never figured her out. She could stand with her back to the class and all of a sudden she'd say, "Graney, pay attention. Stop looking round." Not only me, but the whole class. She'd tell them off for things she could not possibly have seen. She was tagged as a real witch. We kept well out of her way.

I used to dread going to school when I was in her class. I played wag more than once, but it was a serious offence. We had a School Board man, a big tall fellow with a ferocious Kitchener-style moustache, a long black coat and a peaked cap. Oh, he was a terror. But then, the whole system was built on fear, like the ghosts trick they used, to try to keep kids away from mill lodges. Most of the mills were steam-driven and the huge boilers were fed from the lodges. These man-made lakes, unfenced, deep, full of fish, were warm for the occasional swim, because some of the used water was fed back into them. So they held a tremendous fascination for kids. But it was said they were peopled by the ghosts of suicides who had jumped into them. Come dusk, we would be hanging around, looking for their ghosts, and it was quite easy to see them, because as soon as the warm water hit the cooler air, you would have these swirls of drifting vapour, vague wraiths that were anything you wanted them to be, rising from the water.

Those were our childhood monsters. Nothing compared with the real evils that the world would soon be throwing at us, but quite effective in keeping us away from danger. Present-day boggarts are not quite so harmless, of course. They call them town planners.

CHAPTER 3

IRON AND BRASS

Time for a break (photograph Paul Graney).

AFTER we moved to Manchester, the first job I managed to get, when I was nearly 16, was at a little engineering works in Collyhurst. It was run by an old man, Tom Murphy, and had once been fairly thriving, with eight or nine workmen. But now there was only the old chap, and he needed a lad to help him with the rough work.

I'd come straight from the mill and yet I was expected to work a couple of lathes and a big drill press, work on the forge, do both fire and oxy-acetylene welding, work

34

on the bench and produce good results with saw and file. This old chap had been in it since he was a lad and thought anybody should be able to turn something up on the lathe or weld things together in a neat and orderly manner. To some extent he was prepared to show me, but he couldn't really understand why I couldn't work to a couple of 'thous' with a file in a vice. He'd been doing it all his life; it was second nature.

He treated me pretty well, but his standards were those of the 1870s. He had no conception of what things were like outside his workshop. His world was his local pub, his house just across the road in Collyhurst Street, and his workshop. I don't think he'd even been out of the district since about 1880, because he seemed to have no conception of place or time.

He certainly could not comprehend my one big fear. Electricity was still fairly expensive, so he had a big gas engine to work all the machinery. It was 20 or 25 horsepower with a flywheel about six feet across and ten inches wide. Each day I had to start it up, and I would rather have faced a hungry crocodile! It had to be started by hand, using a steel handle sticking out of the flywheel. As soon as it fired, it took off, and the handle with it. I was terrified that I wouldn't let go quickly enough and it would whirl me around. Old Tom didn't try to reassure me – saying it had thrown one of his lads against the wall and crippled him for life!

One of the things we made was church screens, big curlicued ironwork panels with slots for the hymn numbers. Big things, about six feet by four feet. We did them on contract for Baxendales, a big wholesale ironmongers on Miller Street. They were really the ones who put old Murphy out of business, quoting a price and then cutting it back until most of his margin was gone. And he'd fall for it every time.

I've said he had no sense of time or place. Well, on one occasion, we'd made a couple of these screens, about seven or eight hundredweight altogether, all scrolled ironwork. And he said they had to be delivered to a church in Swinton. "Where's that?" I asked.

"Oh, it's in Salford ... you can always ask."

If I'd only known! It was a good six miles away. We did hand cart repairs for a chap who hired them out to the barrow boys, so I borrowed one for nothing and loaded up the screens. The springs flattened out till the handcart body was touching the wheels and at about 9am, I set off to find Swinton.

I'd no money, none at all; thinking Swinton was only in Salford and I'd be back by dinnertime, I'd left my newspaper full of sandwiches in the shop and there I was, wandering around somewhere 'tother end of Salford. I must have gone miles. Anyway, at about 7pm, as the light was fading, a policeman who'd already seen me a couple of times wandering round, asked me where I was going. I told him and he says, you're miles from that church, lad, there'll be nobody there now. So he took me to the police station. They put the cart in the yard and gave me a meal, then got in touch with Murphy. He wasn't even worried. He assumed I'd done the delivery and taken the cart home and would have turned up in the morning.

Anyway, the police gave me a voucher to get home on the bus. I left the cart with the gear there. But they didn't give me a voucher to get back again, so in the morning I had to walk from Regent Square in Salford, collect the cart, get proper directions and eventually find the church. There was nobody there and the gates were locked, but I wasn't going to push the damned lot back home. So I found a bloke who helped me over the railings with the screens and there we left them, propped against the wall. And when I got back, Old Murph was upset that I hadn't got a signature for them!

This was the pattern of work then. I often think, when I see these bright little lads today, these office and shop boys, they think they're roughing it if they have to go to work wearing the same shirt two days on the run.

Old Murphy once sent me to Dunkerley's, an iron founders on Ancoats Lane, to get a bar of iron, about two inches by three-eighths by roughly 21 feet – what they called a random length. It weighed the best part of one hundredweight and the chaps at Dunkerley's – about half an hour's walk away – just gave me the bar of iron, and I signed for it and marched out with it on my shoulder. Marched! My knees buckled under the weight of it.

I didn't find out until later that it was illegal for one man to carry anything that would project round a corner, that it should have been a two-man job, or delivered by lorry. It took me all my time just to walk between the bounces: as the front and back ends touched the ground it bounced up and I took a step; when the ends flexed down again, I waited till it bounced up and took another step. And so on, for two miles. It's a wonder the police didn't stop me. I know everybody was turning round and looking at me, with 21 feet of bouncing iron on my shoulder!

And all Murph said when I got back, was, "I thought they'd have cut it in two for you!" And he was worried that it had taken me so long. Dunkerley's was less than half an hour's walk and I'd taken two and a half. He was a decent old bloke really. Inside his works he was a past master. He could take a lump of iron and practically carve a clock out of it. He knew his job backwards. But in the street, he had no idea.

As for me, I had to learn fast. It was here that I got my first insight into the barrow boys' underworld. A number of them owned their own barrows, and brought them in to be repaired. We'd make new handles and put new floorboards in, as well as all the ironwork needed. I've seen Old Murph build a complete new iron-rimmed wheel, spokes and all. But as often as not he wouldn't get paid. They'd see him right in other ways. He once brought in a big cardboard box and said, "Here you are, take that home." The box contained about 40 pounds of vegetables and fruit: potatoes, cabbages, oranges. One of the lads had left it at his home with his missus.

"There's more than we can eat," he said. "It's like a greengrocer's shop up there!" I was walking from Salford up to Collyhurst at that time because I couldn't afford the bus fares. I think I was getting about eight shillings a week and it would have cost me that in bus fares. I couldn't carry all of it on my shoulders in the cardboard box all that way, so I took it home in small doses.

About the underworld? One time a chap came to us and said, "My barrow wheels have broken, but I've got another pair." Murph did a really good job for him but the bloke said he couldn't pay him right then. "In the meantime," he said, "send your lad with me and I'll give him some fruit for the pair of you to share." So I went with him up Churnet Street, and we were pushing the barrow up a steep hill near the public baths when a chap passing by said: "Them's my bloody wheels you've got on there ... you've pinched 'em!" An argument started, so I whipped into the doorway of the baths.

Within minutes, the street was full of people fighting.

This chap shouted one or two of his mates down, and the chap I was with called some of his pals, and it ended up with a battle royal, about 40 blokes fighting with broken bottles and sticks and half bricks. I was terrified. I scrunched up in the doorway. It was like a film, except I was in the middle of it. There were bricks flying and blokes kept running past me and staring at me as if I was on the wrong side. Nobody set into me though, probably because I was so young and not taking any part. I've been in a lot of trouble since, but I've never forgotten that battle.

It was my first experience of the Manchester gangs, the Churnet Street gang, the Collyhurst gang, and the James Old gang. With us doing their repairs, I got to know quite a lot of them and long after I'd left there, they'd remember me, give me an apple or orange and say how do. I felt rather proud that all these rough types who were in and out of jail, accepted me as somebody they would speak to. My pals probably thought it was a bit rum, though.

And it all stemmed from Murphy's, where I did in fact get a fair grounding in engineering. But as I said earlier, Mr Murphy eventually went bust. He'd never codge a job, whether it was some little girl's doll's pram needed mending, or a housewife with a broken metal picture frame, even though he knew he'd probably be paid in oranges, or not at all. A really decent old chap in the bottom of him. But the final straw was Baxendales' vicious undercutting.

So he eventually petered out, and I was back on the dole, one of the few occasions I was legally on it and didn't lose the first six weeks. Usually when I'd come out of a job, I'd done or said something and been sacked or quit and got my dole stopped. This was the pattern of my life. But Murphy's was a good grounding.

Eventually I got a job at a garage, R G Turner's of Brunswick Street. It's all demolished now and become part of the University. I was only just turned 16, but on the strength of my experience at Murph's, this chap with a little engineering works down New York Street, decided I was clever enough to make some oil gauges that he'd invented.

He put me in a corner of his workshop. First I had to knurl these brass rods in the lathe. They were about five eighths of an inch in diameter, and I had to turn brass knobs out of them, parting them off, as it's known. Then I had to drill a hole through the centre of them and cut and stamp the gauge itself, a thin strip of iron with numbers stamped along it at the proper intervals. Then I had to solder the iron strips into the brass knobs and fit them into steel tubes which had to be tapped at one end and screwed at the other. Quite a complicated process.

They seemed to be selling well and this was about the first period in my life when I really began to look closely at the class structure. He got me an assistant, quite a well-spoken young lad, with a bib and brace overall. First they got him a white linen apron to keep his overalls clean, then he made himself a sacking apron to keep his linen apron clean.

I should have known! He was frightened of the lathe, because he didn't want to get his hands cut. He wouldn't use the drill because it had once spun him round; and he couldn't be trusted to stamp the strips of iron in the right places – that called for a degree of concentration beyond the limits of this grammar school boy. He had to put a mark on the iron opposite the mark on the gauge and that was also beyond his comprehension. He wouldn't assemble them, because it made his hands dirty with oil, and he wouldn't solder the brass knobs on because he was frightened of getting burned. So all in all, he used to just stooge about, watching me.

Well, the boss came down one day, and this lad was immediately busy putting the finished gauges in boxes. "I've given you someone to help," said the boss. "I've doubled your staff but you've not doubled your output. Why not?" I'd been brought up not to snitch to the boss, no matter what, so I just said, "Well?" Luckily, the foreman had seen all this going on and he gave the game away. He said, "I'll tell you why not. It's because this fellow here is an idle little illegitimate! You're wasting any money you're paying him." But of course they didn't sack him; they took him across to the garage and found him a job in the office. He did eventually leave, but he wasn't sacked, because his father played golf with our boss and they were members of the same secret societies.

The soldering was done across at the garage, where they were a pretty rough lot. Soon enough, they started talking about an initiation. Well, I'd had enough of that in the mill. These garage types had sent one lad home without his trousers. The day came and they shouted after me as I went up the stairs: "We'll be up for you in a few minutes."

There was a big zinc bath there, full of dirty water in which hot metal had been dipped. I dragged it over to the door and when I heard someone coming up the stairs I opened the door and tipped the lot down – all over the boss! Back at the Labour Exchange, they said I had been guilty of misconduct and I had the dole stopped for six weeks.

By this time, somebody had given me an old typewriter which I'd fettled up and I was doing bits of wall newspaper for a club I'd been going to, and I was thinking of trying to write something. Then I saw an advert in a newspaper: 'Work at home typewriting'. I was a hunt and peck merchant, one finger on each hand, but I thought, it's at home, nobody will know. So I went to this place, a solicitor's office in Fountain Street, near Lewis's.

Dickens would have had a heyday with it. You sat on high stools at sloping desks. I was nearly six feet tall and even my feet were off the ground. And what characters! They all wore black suits, narrow trousers, winged collars. I could scarcely credit it, but there they were, and they handed me a couple of telephone directories and a box of envelopes, and said, "Right, we've ticked off every address in the telephone directories that we want typing on the envelopes."

So I thought, I can manage that, and asked, "What do you pay?" Seven shillings and sixpence a thousand! I was two finger typing for seven days from about nine in the morning till about half-past ten at night. Monday afternoon I took them back and got my seven shillings and sixpence. I did another lot just to get some money, and then they said they could find me a regular job for nine or ten shillings a week.

I expected to get similar typing work but instead was given a ledger and told to copy it in handwriting. My writing is the well-known inky spider walk. It was agony. Then on the second morning, this long, lanky character, with a face like a bottle of vinegar, sauntered up to my desk and said, "Are those the best clothes you've got?"

"They're the *only* clothes I've got."

"Well," he says, "they won't do for here, you've got to dress better than that."

"Alright, when I get some money."

"Well," he said, "you can't get money until you've worked for it."

"Well then, I can't get better clothes, and on what you're paying me it'll be a bloody long time before I do!"

Back at the Labour Exchange, I found there was no work again and I got stopped dole for a further six weeks, for leaving my job voluntarily.

It was one of the quirks of the time that a large proportion of the jobs advertised called for a strong youth, which meant you had to be between 16 and 17, strong and tall, with all the physical ability and skills of a man. What they really wanted was a tradesman for a youth's wage, 18 shillings instead of two pounds. I missed many a job because I didn't have the requisite skills. Manchester then was full of cotton warehouses and I applied at many of them as a packer and folder, or inspector, but fell foul of this strong youth with skill gimmick.

The best-off blokes seemed to be the unofficial work force, the handcart wallahs who hung around the back-street loading bays with a cart they'd hired for a shilling a day. They had jealously-guarded regular places, and you would see them trotting merrily down the back streets, piled up with huge bolts of cloth, delivering from one warehouse to another. They were all better off than your average workman; some small shopkeepers didn't make as much.

But I couldn't break into it, so I got into the printing business, in a way. It was an odd sort of job, in a place at the corner of the old City Road and Medlock Street, right opposite the gasworks. It made destination screens for the trams. In case it's not generally known, they didn't print white letters on a black background, they printed the background and left the letters white. The printing pad was linen, such as you could get then, from which they cut out the letter shapes. Then when the pad – it could be about two feet six inches by three feet – was inked and put through the appropriate mangle, it printed everything in black, leaving the letters white.

It wasn't a big firm. There was the boss and a woman who stitched a selvedge on the ends of the six-foot screens, and four lads, two on nights and two on days. You took a week on days and a week on nights. It was donkey work. The bleached white linen was put on a roll to be fed through the mangle, which was about five feet wide with steel rollers and a big handle. Next to this was a table about 20 yards long, on which one of you inked the pads, using a gelatine roller that weighed about 20 pounds, and printer's ink which was kept bubbling on a stove.

We got a guinea [*one pound one shilling*] a week. This was fairly average for a youth, because after all deductions, you were just sixpence, or one shilling above the dole level. Naturally, they claimed you could bump it up with overtime. Oh dear! If you were on day shift and worked till 10pm from an 8am start you'd made yourself a couple of hours overtime. No premium time – it was all straight rates, even if you did the regular 30-odd-hour weekend shift.

And it was a really dirty job. You got covered in printer's ink and there were no special detergents or barrier creams then. You soaked a bit of rag in paraffin and rubbed until you were an even pale grey. Then you started with bath brick and pumice stone and soap.

A factory inspector arrived one day and insisted the boss provided proper hot water and soap and towels. The boss was quite upset because he was very tight with money. I'll say this for him, he never used to dock us for the two-minute silence on Armistice Day, but he didn't like this. He was forced to do it though, and after we got one towel between us and the cheapest, non-lathering yellow bar of soap you can imagine, he started trimming our pay by sixpence a week, to cover the cost.

Not satisfied with that, he then wanted to increase production, but couldn't figure out how to do it because everything was timed, you couldn't speed it up. It worried him to death. He kept throwing out hints that he was going to increase our hours, but by this time the 48-hour week was more or less the legal maximum.

But lots of changes were on the horizon, because 1926 was coming up – the year of the General Strike.

CHAPTER 4

STRIKE!

Heave away (photograph Paul Graney).

WHAT led up to the 1926 General Strike is not really for me to say. The average person knew very little. The newspapers, even the *Daily Herald*, never gave any inside information. You could never find out what was going on, particularly from the standard press: the *Mail*, the *Express*, the *Mirror* and so on. The *Daily Herald* did slightly favour the workers' point of view but it didn't come out with the full story, and of course the *Daily Worker* did not emerge till about 1930.

All we knew was that everybody was going to stop work sometime. It came on 3 May and it was like the end of the world; the Government mobilised as though for war. They commandeered the parks and stationed military vehicles in them, light tanks, reconnaissance cars and army lorries for shifting troops. Tents went up and there were soldiers everywhere.

The first day, it didn't really bite. I don't think anybody believed that it would really work, although there was a complete power blackout until the Government put the troops into the power stations.

But on the second day there was a complete transport stoppage. Most people had neither seen nor envisaged anything like it. Those who didn't own a bicycle started walking into Manchester to work. I knew someone who walked in from Hyde and some made it from as far out as Altrincham, seven or eight miles. Mind you, people were more used to walking then. Nowadays not many people walk for pleasure and they won't walk to the next bus stop.

Some firms put camp beds in their offices, but this was frowned upon. I remember the BBC commenting on it, hinting about amateur brothels. They didn't actually say brothels, that was a dirty word, but they talked about the immorality of having men and women sleeping in the same building. Cafes and hotels made a fortune. They would have liked it to go on for ever. There were queues outside the cafes, with people trying to buy ready-made meals, and the hotels were full of businessmen and the top boys in industry who were living close to their factories, trying to keep them going.

After the first couple of days, the TUC had promised to keep the hospitals supplied, but it didn't really work. So the Government got volunteers to provide food and essential supplies to hospitals and old people's homes. I think there was some sort of deal between the Government and the TUC. But the pickets didn't discriminate. If they saw a lorry moving, they would stop it and haul the driver out and no amount of chits from the TUC would prevent them from either emptying the lorry or immobilising it. So the Government started putting armed troops in the lorries, with orders to shoot if trouble arose. This really alienated the Government from the workers, who realised just how little power they had outside election time.

I had no need to strike, but I did. All four of us at the screen printers did, more for a holiday than anything else. But of course it was all unpaid. The day of the closed shop was a long way off. A lot of places wouldn't employ you if you were in a union. Anyway, we marched out, the four of us. What the sewing woman did, I can't remember. We left the boss there on his own.

I was involved in various political activities at the time. On and off, when I'd been unemployed, I'd been on various unemployed workers' committees and this led to me being right in the middle of organising the General Strike pickets. Picketing was rough. If the police came you had only to be standing outside a works, and they would wade in, truncheons swinging. They didn't tell you to move, they didn't do anything except rush at you and try to beat you on the skull, and if they could wrestle you to the ground, then it was handcuffs on and you'd be marched to the station, accused of obstruction, violence to the police, all the crimes you could be charged with.

So I made some suggestions and helped to organise the strike along army or police lines. First, we got so many pickets to a firm, according to its size. Then we would let them stay there for perhaps only two hours. If it was reasonably free from police interruption, they might stay all morning. Then they would move on to another firm. We ensured a constant circulation of pickets, so that the same faces weren't on show for too long and the police wouldn't get to know us.

We had a corps of bicycle riders taking messages between groups. If the police smashed up one lot of pickets and scattered them, or beat them down, a bicycle rider watching from a distance would ride to tell the central committee, which in our case was in a house just off Chester Road, and we'd get another set of pickets down there fast. We were covering part of Trafford Park and some of the chain of industries on Ordsall Lane, from Regent Road to Trafford Road: the Co-op tea place, Dicky Howarth's mill, the dye works, all the engineering places at the back, and Happy Annie's, the Hamilton and Woods engineers.

So it was organised, all over Manchester, all over the country, outside the TUC, by ordinary blokes like myself.

And of course we became the 'Reds'. The Russians had organised us and subsidised us! We couldn't raise the price of a pint between us, but the Russians were subsidising us and organising it all, which was the cry for everything then, particularly from the *Mail* and the *Express*.

At the end of the strike, the *Daily Mail* headlines were on the lines of Surrender of the Revolutionaries – a Triumph for the People! It declared that Zenovia, the Russian bogeyman, had planned the strike in 1918, and that between 500 and 1,000 Soviet agents had fomented it. Dissolve the TUC and clear out the Soviets, it said. You had only to come out of work those days to become a Russian agent and learn the cry: "Go back to Russia!"

But during the strike it was mostly rumours. The printers came out, and most of the papers were trying to get out papers printed by their managements. The *Daily*

Herald printers, though, managed to produce a daily quarter sheet: Justice for the Miners; Labour's One Aim; Blame Rests on the Government; Beware of the Wireless – The Government Controls It! Every day the same headlines. There was a Government broadsheet called the *British Gazette*, run by Winston Churchill. The *Daily Mail* had a two-page issue printed in Paris and flown over. Their headlines of course were always: For King and Country; A Pistol at the Nation's Head; Send Them Back To Russia!

But there was no real way of telling the people anything. Nothing could be believed on either side. So everybody came out on strike. The unions were working through their trades union branch secretaries, giving instructions by word of mouth. People who didn't belong to the unions just waited for something to happen.

In the meantime, all the ill-feeling was bubbling up. On one occasion, I was in Hyde Road outside the tram depot. The trams couldn't come out because of the lack of power, but a few single-decker buses were rolling out, manned by university students, mainly middle and upper class kids having a big adventure as strike-breakers. I saw many a one stopped and those silly kids dragged out and beaten up. They usually handed them over to the women, and they were a lot rougher than the men. Men would probably have given them a punch on the nose and kicked their behinds up the street, but the women, oh dear, the women gave 'em hell. There must have been about 40 or 50 women. Some lay on the road outside the depot and when a bus stopped, they'd drag a lad out and hand him over to the beating-up squad.

Finally dozens of men and women got on one side of a bus in an archway leading from the depot and rocked it until it tipped on its side and stopped any more getting out. They were trying the same thing at another entrance when the police arrived, smashing about with their clobber sticks, so I decided it was time I was somewhere else.

One brush I had with the police was outside a place I've already mentioned, Hamilton and Woods, an engineering shop employing 300 or 400 people, between the River Irwell and Ordsall Lane. It's been demolished a long while now but there were half a dozen like it nearby. They were hell holes. Two or three of my pals worked there and it was known euphemistically as Happy Annie's. It was one of the firms that paid just sixpence more than the dole. In those days you had to take a job if it was offered, or have your dole stopped.

Consequently, Annie's was full of really desperate people. They'd been out of work for years, their families were starving. They were fighting to get in, and we were trying to persuade them to stay out, but they'd been without money for so long, they wouldn't take any notice of us. Married men coming out with seventeen shillings and sixpence a week, it was pathetic to see them. Many a time I've talked about this and I've seen the look of utter disbelief on people's faces.

Well there we were this morning. All we had were placards hung around our waists, DON'T BREAK THE STRIKE, COME OUT WITH US and such like. We were just standing there. We didn't even speak to those blokes as they went in. We just let them see the placards. The works was surrounded on three sides by a warren of little side streets and three-foot-wide back entries. And suddenly, from all these little streets and entries, the police boiled out. Must have been 40 or 50 of them, though there were only six of us. We had had it more or less planned, but our tactics didn't work. We were going to go one down here, and one down there, scatter, but there were ten policemen to every one of us.

My particular escape route was through the works next door and I don't think they had allowed for this. They'd corked up every street and entry but hadn't allowed for anybody shooting down the factory yard. I dashed into the empty factory, out through a window at the back, then along the Irwell towpath, to come up at Regent Bridge. I think I was the only one that got away. The others got well pasted. One bloke lost an eye, hit with a truncheon. They were all kept in clink overnight and fined the following morning.

Another brush with the police, this time rather remote, was in Trafford Park. We were picketing Kilverts, the lard company, in Trafford Road at the entrance to the Park, at a point where two or three sets of the Park's own train lines ran alongside the road. There were about seven of us standing outside the main gates. We had orders to allow only so many in, just enough to supply food for hospitals and old folks' homes.

Our chap on crow, the look-out, gave us the whistle that the police were on their way. So we scattered across the road, where there was a big engineering firm, Lancashire Dynamo and Motor Company. We had planned a way out down the two sides of this building, which would lead us past the Co-op flour mills and on to the Manchester side of the docks, but when we looked round, Harry Potkin was missing.

I'd better tell you about Harry. He was a madman of the first water. I don't know why he was in the strike movement at all because at 18 he was self-employed. He'd bolted an ordinary piano on to a handcart, and would stop in the middle of a street, jump up and start playing. He was quite a good pub-type pianist, playing by ear, but he could knock out a good tune. I was coming down Medlock Street once, and stopped to watch him. He played his tunes during the day, including a couple of waltzes for the old dears, then went knocking on doors and got something at most of them. Even if it was only a penny, he must have earned two or three shillings for half an hour's work.

So if he did five or six performances a day, he could earn nearly a pound a day. No stoppages, all clear profit. And the handcart and piano were his own. And I was working for less than a pound a week. Mind you, he had to contend with wind and weather, I suppose. Anyway, whatever his reasons, he was out picketing with us. But when we split up, each party thought he was with the other. We all hid as soon as we could and looked back. There stood the police in a row, leaning against some railway wagons. And there too, was Potkin, underneath the wagons with a tin of red paint and a little brush, painting the backs of their shoe heels.

They caught him of course. He'd done about a dozen shoes when he was spotted. They hauled him out and after a good thumping wheeled him off to Northumberland Street police station at Old Trafford. Oh, the charges they threw at him! The only ones I can remember now are damaging Government property, which was painting the coppers' shoes; incitement to riot, because he'd been picketing; and subversive activities. They brought him up the next morning and he was fined between £40 and £50. He hadn't a cat in hell's chance of paying, so he went to jail for two months, and when he came out he was a sort of folk hero around Hulme: here comes Potkin with his can of paint! He revelled in it.

In the meantime, Metro Vicks, at the top end of Trafford Park, was having it rough. Metropolitan Vickers, to give it its full name, employed several thousand people, and both before and after this, right up to the War breaking out, it was a hotbed of dissension. All the evil little stunts they could pull on workmen and apprentices, they did. There were hundreds of people outside every entrance, lots of police too and the meetings were ending in pitched battles and scores of arrests, fines and prison sentences. It was like the revolution had come, except that the workers stood no chance.

It's a good job the General Strike lasted only nine days, because by about the fifth day, people were already going hungry. There was no food to be had. The shops had been raided in the early days. People with any money had stocked up, having had a good bit of advance warning, and the shops had been emptied of the staples. Flour, sugar, butter, margarine, jam and all the tinned stuff had disappeared in a frenzy of panic buying. The poor people of course didn't have enough money to join in. They were struggling, going hungry, and they didn't know when it would end.

Somebody in our section, the Hulme section, had a relation who worked on the canal boats, and he'd been told that a lot of eggs and lettuce and various other foodstuffs were on a barge coming from the Fylde, the big plain between Preston, Morecambe and Blackpool, famous for its eggs, potatoes and market gardening. The Bridgewater Canal was built for that traffic as well as coal. The boats came into Potato Wharf, near Liverpool Street [*on the Manchester/Salford boundary*]. The food was all intended for hospitals but our informant suspected that it was going to the wrong people, the black market brigade, so he passed the word to our strike committee.

We borrowed lots of kids' sugar-box handcarts and hired all the full-size handcarts we could, then set off one midnight. We had to go down into Salford, round the bottom of Dawson Street, past the abattoir, and along the narrow lane that led to Potato Wharf. And in no time we emptied that barge – I don't think we left a lettuce leaf.

Then somebody came along. Not a watchman, but a bloke who lived on a coal barge in Bridgewater Wharf nearby. We told him about the black market and he said, "I've a load of coal probably going to the same place. If you can get into it, me and the wife are going to see her mother ..."

We only half emptied that one, because it could be seen from Deansgate, but we unloaded a few tons off it, and took it round when we distributed the food. We saw that the old people and those with families got a couple of buckets each. We would have got 99 years if they'd caught us.

After nine days, ten if you count the Sunday, the strike was called off, but the miners, who had worked with the TUC only as long as it refused to consider wage reductions, broke away when they found it was doing just that. The TUC called the General Strike off on 13 May, but the miners stayed out. They were still out as winter came on; they were really desperate. Unions and workers' organisations were trying to help, sending food parcels, helping miners they knew, feeding and clothing the kids, giving money to mining neighbours, but it wasn't enough.

Some miners were driven to sheep rustling, going up into the hills and killing sheep to bring home and share out. It was a truly desperate time for them. A lot left the industry and many went abroad, thousands of them to Australia and South Africa. I don't really think they recovered from that 1926 strike until modern times.

As for me, the General Strike cost me my screen-printing job. We had all walked out as I said earlier, and after it was all over the boss said, "We don't need Bolsheviks like you." That was the favourite word for Communists. The battle in Russia had been between the Bolsheviks and the Mensheviks. I found out later that all the word Bolsheviks meant was majority, and Mensheviks meant minority. But in Britain, if you didn't fit the social or political norm, you were automatically a Bolshevik and the same phrase was shouted then as is shouted now: "Go back to Russia!"

The boss didn't exactly sack us, but he took on a couple more blokes and we were gradually eased out. It didn't worry me overmuch, losing a dirty, hard, underpaid job like that, with long hours and hardly any leisure time. Even when I got time off I was too exhausted to use it.

So it was back to the Labour Exchange. They were beginning to know me by then, like they knew so many others.

CHAPTER 5

TRICKS AND NO TRADE

Paul at work.

I WAS out of work another few months, dodging about. But just before my six months ran out, which would have meant the Means Test, I managed to get a job at an ornamental ironworks in Hulme. They made gates, railings and big screens. It was typical of its day and exploited its workers like all the other firms.

There were about 30 lads round about my age: helpers' mates. We were paid the usual wage of about one pound one shilling, which after stoppages brought us down to the usual ninepence, or one shilling above the dole money. There were very few apprentices and they got only about five shillings a week. Even in the last of their five years, they'd be getting less than a labourer's one pound a week.

As soon as they had finished their time, passed their exams and got their papers, they were sacked – a wonderful scheme for cheap labour. Mind you, the rest of us never learned a trade, so we could never get a job as a skilled man.

It was a rough place, and these lads, not caring about the job very much, used to get up to all sorts of stunts, and although I was involved in one or two, I usually got blamed for a lot that I wasn't involved in.

The toilets in an engineering works in those days, or in any kind of works, were very primitive. Putting toilets in was the last thing anybody thought of. I can remember these in particular. They were in an upstairs room of the workshop, behind a rough partition. No women worked in the place, and the partition wasn't very important; it just covered one corner. They'd built a row of wooden cubicles to cover the toilets. The doors started about 15 inches or so off the floor and were cut off at about five feet. This was because there was no smoking in the works. It wasn't really important or necessary, as there was nothing that would catch fire easily. I think they could get a cheaper insurance premium if there was no smoking allowed. So of course they just banned smoking and saved themselves a pound or two on the premiums.

So all the compulsive smokers used to disappear into the toilets, for a fag, and naturally the lads would skive off up there too, as often as they could.

Then the chargehand would come looking for them. He would walk along checking which ones were occupied, and what kind of feet were at the bottom, then he'd look over the top to see if it was one of his lads, then he'd have him out. That's what the toilets were designed for, so that you could be hauled out of them easily by the chargehand.

But these kids – I'm saying kids, I was one of 'em, 16, 18 – would push a piece of angle iron about ten feet long through the handles of the toilet doors, locking in four or five in one go. Then they'd go along with big bundles of lighted newspapers and shove 'em under the doors. Think about it – you're sitting there meditating about what you will wear at Ascot this year, when a sheet of flame shoots up at you. It disturbs the concentration somewhat. It's also very difficult jumping up on to the seat and trying to get over the top of the door with your pants round your ankles. It wasn't very popular this stunt.

In the big bottom workshop, fitting benches lined the two outside walls where the windows were. The window ledges were just below bench level and the fitters would reach over and put their baggings [*wrapped lunches*] there. There was no canteen, just a geyser for brewing up, across the road in the paint shop. Each fitter would use his own section of the window ledge more or less as a locker. That's where he put his brew can and his sandwiches wrapped in newspaper.

One of the lads' other tricks was to crawl along under the bench, snaffle as many packets of sandwiches as possible, replace the meat, or the cheese and pickle with thick lubricating grease, and put them back very carefully. I got blamed a couple of times for this, though I didn't even know it was going on at first. The manager had me in the office with one or two others and we had to agree to a stoppage in our wages to pay for the sandwiches they said we'd ruined.

Then there was the bowler hat episode. There was a whole pecking order in head-gear. A man working a drill press wasn't as high up in the hierarchy as an assembler, so he would go to work in a cap. The top trades, who worked to blueprints, fitting the whole job together, wore a bowler as a badge of office. No one else was allowed to come to work in one.

Near the main gate was an enormous room. It contained a table easily 20 yards long and 10 yards wide, on which gates and railings were assembled. And all along the wall of this assembly room was the cloakroom – a series of six inch nails knocked into the wall. Of course the hierarchy, all the elite, had their coats and bowler hats hanging together in a row.

One week, the council was macadamising the road nearby, covering up all the old cobbles. The boiler was in a side street, and some bright lads brought a bucket to work, filled it with hot tar, then poured tar into each bowler and put it back on its nail. By evening the macadam had set solid. If the building was still there, those hats would still be stuck on that wall.

And, of course, there was hell to pay. I was living a life of virtuous innocence. Just one bunch got up to all this hell raising and I knew nothing about it – until I went for my wages. I think I was about a shilling and sixpence short, quite an amount for that period. "Go to the pay office and tell them," said the chargehand. The chap in the office called in one of the big chiefs, who, very quietly and politely said, "Follow me, lad." Back across the road, he said, "Get me one of those bowler hats off its nail, will you?" And of course it was stuck solid.

"That's what you're paying for," he said. "We've stopped wages out of every lad in the shop to pay for new hats."

I tried arguing. We had no union, but I threatened the law and I did in fact go to the town hall to see my councillor. He said he would come and see my boss, and he kept his word. It was like a tribunal. The boss said, "We don't know who did it, so we stopped the lot."

The councillor said, "You can't do that. You're allowed to get the money back, but not off innocent people."

The upshot was that they had to return my money. But after the councillor had gone, the boss said, "I know your type. You're a trouble-maker, a bother-causer." And I was transferred down the road, to the firm's leaded light and stained glass factory. I soon found out why. The work was dangerous because you were handling lead all the time. Somebody told me we were entitled to a pint of milk a day to combat the effects of lead colic. But one old chap who had been there for years, said, "Well, I get the milk, but the colic has to put you in hospital first."

So there I was, handling raw lead, melting it and putting it through machines to make the calms: the grooved lengths of lead that hold the pieces of stained glass. I was washing my hands a dozen times a day. I was frightened to death of it because, as this old fellow told me, it had taken most of his stomach out and half his intestines. He was living on milk and fish.

While I was there I got another stoppage in my wages. The swine of a Cockney foreman told me to go the pay office, back at the main works. Once again I was taken to the assembly room. It was here that they used to get the brews ready in the cans and then put them all in a row along the edge of the big table where the assemblers worked. When the buzzer went, they just grabbed their can and ran like hell to the geyser across the road in the paint shop. The break was short and there was only one tap to brew from, so it was a matter of the quickest runner.

Anyway, all the brew cans were lined up on the bench, and the boss said, "Get me one of those, will you?" You guessed? Yes, some bright spark had nailed them all to the bench. "Well," I said, "I don't know whether you remember the last time when I brought the councillor in about the bowler hats. I'm working down at Lucy Street now, at the leaded light place. I've had no chance to do this, and I'm quite prepared to bring somebody in again." So I got my money back.

But I didn't always win. It wasn't actually by explosives, but I was blown up a couple of times. There was a big cast iron melting pot in the works, about two feet six inches deep and the same width, with a big gas flame under it. Everything went into it, including scrap lead bought from demolition merchants. Often it was old pipes hammered over at each end. I had to chisel them open to let any water out. But it doesn't need much. Your boiler might be half full of molten lead and then you chuck a piece in that's just wet, and bang, the whole lot goes up.

The pot had a tin shield round it, but it would just blow that over, and you'd find yourself with two or three hundredweight of molten lead dripping off the ceiling. Once when I got blown up, I was off work for a fortnight. Molten lead had fallen off the ceiling, badly burning my back. I tried to get compensation, but I got nothing, not even my wages. There was no union to fight my cause and the solicitor I went to said, "All it is is burns. If you were scarred, we could perhaps get you a few pounds."

"But what about my loss of wages?"

"Oh," he said, "you can forget that."

The way I lost that job was another time when I was the innocent bystander – more or less. Down in the bottom where I worked was another firm who made artificial floors. One of the chemicals they used was called Magnetite which looked like transparent soda crystals. One of the workers gave me a matchboxful. "Just one crystal in a pot of tea ... it's tasteless ... and whoever drinks that tea won't get off the bog for a month," he laughed.

That's handy, I thought. Then I did a stupid thing. I gave the matchbox to Col, a mad so-and-so who worked upstairs. He was about 40 and I was 19. And the first thing he did was put a little piece in the Cockney foreman's tea. Well, he stayed locked in his own little private toilet all the afternoon. Then he was off for three days and Mad Col gave him another dose. This time he had to see a doctor and they traced it back to the chemical. And it came back to me and I copped for all the blame.

I suppose it was only justice. This time I did get the sack and it was back to, "Have you worked since you last signed?"

Again.

CHAPTER 6

DOLE DAYS

THE days of the dole – between two and three million idle good-for-nothing layabouts were roaming Britain. At least this is what the media called them, and anybody who had not yet had the happy experience of trying to extract a few shillings a week out of a labour bureau, automatically agreed. I know men, even today, who for one reason or another are lucky enough never to have been out of work, who still maintain that nobody needed to have been unemployed – that they must have been idle.

In the 1920s I think the dole for a grown man was 15 shillings a week and by about 1929 it had risen to 17 shillings and sixpence. Even taking into account the cheapness of goods, it went nowhere. But when people complained, they were told the country was bankrupt and that anyway, the dole wasn't supposed to be a wage, it was only meant to keep you alive until you got a job. You might be kept alive, but you certainly could not thrive on it.

There were always plenty of police on duty at the Manchester dole queues, which, at Aytoun Street stretched, four deep, all the way to Piccadilly Gardens, in spite of a so-called staggered system. You were issued with a yellow card from the Labour Exchange to prove that you were an authentic, good-for-nothing layabout, and on it was marked a signing-on time. Wednesdays and Fridays were signing on days, and you were given one of the quarter of an hour slots. But with the usual Civil

Service efficiency there would probably be 60 or 70 men allotted to each quarter hour. There were scores of clerks at long desks and you all had your own clerk: "Box number three, nine forty-five." If you had not been seen within 15 minutes, you had to return after 4pm. Of course, you would usually find hundreds still waiting outside and you still didn't get seen. So you had to return the following day.

Naturally, tempers got frayed and there was a lot of argument. It was like something out of Dickens, the clerks more like prison guards. They never spoke to you civilly, just snarled: "Have you worked since you last signed?" This was the formula, the ritual you had to go through. Twice a week you had to tell them you hadn't worked since you last signed. It was printed too, on your yellow layabout's card. The clerk had to ask it and you had to say "No". You couldn't shake your head. Some clerks, although I never came across one, insisted on, "No, sir". I wish one had tried it on me! You had to be careful, though. Just look wrong at one of them and you could be up before a tribunal and a tribunal could knock your dole off.

If you left your job, you got six weeks' dole stopped; the same if you were sacked for misconduct. There were several ways to lose the dole and it could prove a real tragedy. They were just phasing out the Poor Law Guardians at that time and it seemed the only way to get money from the new National Assistance Board, was to be married with twelve kids. If you were single and tried to get anything, you were just shown the door.

So it was as well to be very circumspect with some of these little monsters behind the dole counters, secure in their own jobs. There was a lot of ill-feeling. A lot of them were dragged across the counter and bobbed on the nose by people who had been taunted to desperation. It wasn't long before they doubled the width of the counters so they were out of reach.

They had all sorts of little schemes and dodges to get you off the dole. At one stage they gave us all little notebooks and we had to get twelve signatures or work stamps a week, from firms we'd applied to for a job. But when you went to the lodge keeper or gateman and asked for a signature, he might already have signed or stamped 50 that day. Naturally the firms got fed up with it and not long ago it was still possible to see some of the old notices at factory entrances: 'Applicants for employment MUST apply at the Labour Exchange.'

Around 1930, when I was 20, I had my first long stint on the dole. After six months on the dole, drawing your fabulous wealth, you automatically went before a tribunal, usually a bunch of businessmen, who worked the infamous Means Test, questioning you very severely about your efforts to get work. They knew perfectly well that not one firm in 10,000 would employ somebody off the street, but they insisted on seeing your bookful of signatures. They wanted to know who lived in your house, who was working and how much they earned. Then you would be asked to come back the next week.

During that week, a type of bailiff would call at the house. The one that called at ours really frightened my mother with his arrogant sergeant-major attitude. I said, "Here, just a minute, I'm the one that's having the tribunal. Talk to me." He ignored me, eyeing the piano someone had given my mother years before. "That could go," he said and noted it down in his book. "You'd get fifteen pound for that." In reality we couldn't have got 15 shillings! "The three piece suite could go too. You don't need luxuries, you can have those when you're working." I forget how much he said that was worth, ten pounds or so, but a junk man wouldn't have given us more than a few shillings.

We had a couple of bronze ornamental Marley Horses, a gift my mother had kept since her wedding. "Yes," he said, "those would fetch a couple of pounds."

"I'm not selling those!" cried my mother.

"You'll have to if I say so," he said.

I was beginning to bubble, trying to keep my temper. Then he started to go upstairs, so I barred his way: "You're not going up there."

"Why, what are you hiding up there?"

"Well the first thing I'm hiding is my self-respect. If I let people like you trample around the bedrooms it's time to call it a draw and that's the end of it."

"Okay!" he said as he left. "You've done yourself in!"

And I had. When I went to the tribunal, I was told, "You might have got a little money, not the full dole, but a little money, except for your attitude towards our inspector." So I said I would rather do without the money and keep my self respect. I wasn't having ignorant old men like him tramping round our bedrooms. "So you can stick your money where your love lies," or words to that effect. At this, they called in the sergeant-at-arms, or whatever he was, the bloke with the peaked cap and brass buttons, and debated whether they should have me put in court for using obscene language. "I haven't used any bad language," I said, "so you'd better be sure of your ground."

They let me go.

I suppose I was lucky. The attitude fostered by the

media practically made it a criminal offence to be jobless, setting one half of the country against the other. When you met a stranger, who happened to be working, or somebody with his own business, and you said you were out of work, you could almost see them cringe and back off, as though you'd got leprosy. It even came between friends. If three or four were together and only one was working, he couldn't afford to pay for everybody. So if he went to the pictures or wanted a drink, he would have to do it secretly without his mates. It really split people up.

Meanwhile, I was picking up an odd bob or two here and there, writing articles and short stories for various magazines. Not much, it was a very difficult world to break into and there were many better-educated people than me doing the same thing. But I was picking up an odd bit, and I was learning my way around words, so I smelled a rat when they started sending very cunningly-phrased letters to those of us who had been means tested.

They suggested that we might like to consider enrolling for a scheme whereby we could get a job, provided we had the right qualifications. We had to report to Room 72 at the Brew – our name for the Labour Exchange, or Labour Bureau, as it was also known. Of course, if you didn't enrol, there was a veiled threat in the small print. In my case this turned out to be not having my unemployment insurance card rubber stamped by the dole office. I am now a pensioner and I'm losing more than two pounds a week because I was short of those stamps before the war.

Anyway, we all went to this room 72, about 20 of us, and it was the usual Civil Service, dole, army-type thing, get you there about three o'clock and come out for you about half past four. In the meantime there would be about three or four of these types wandering through: "What are you doing here? Wait outside!"

"We've been told to wait here."

"Who by?"

How were we to know? After about an hour and a half we were called into the room where a well-dressed, well-fed bloke with a suitable accent, setting him apart from all us back street wallahs, gave us a long talk about Canada, what a beautiful place it was. A real travelogue, complete with photographs. "Now we can set you up in your own business. If you're willing to work hard and to do it right, you can have your own farm there."

Wonderful! You had to work for two years for a farmer on spending money pay and then if he gave a good report on you, the Government would give you a grant of land and a small amount of money to set you up. You could build your own house on the land and clear it, and they would give you a couple of hundred dollars to feed you until your got crops growing. They made it sound attractive, but I remembered a lad I'd known at the printing place, who had already been on this scheme. He had been sent to a farm a couple of hundred miles from its nearest neighbour, right out amongst the mountains and a two-day horseback ride to the nearest town. He worked seven days a week from dawn to dusk and slept in the barn's hayloft. He was not allowed to enter the farmhouse under any pretext. He had to knock on the cookhouse door at the back and they gave him a tin plate with food and a mug of coffee. He took this back to the barn to eat it, and that's the way he lived. Hard graft.

A lot of the farmers were notorious for it, according to what he told us. They were given these out-of-work lads from England, and just worked them to death – unpaid labour. They gave them all the heavy work, and ran the feet off them. Anyway, after about twelve months the whole family went to the Calgary Stampede, the big rodeo, and took him along. While he was there he met a couple of English blokes in the same situation. They decided to skip, and after one or two episodes hiding from the police they managed to cross the border into America, only to find thousands there already on the bum because of the Depression.

By judicious night riding and sticking to lonely roads, they managed to avoid the police for about six months. They did transient work, following the crops, and one even worked for a time on a trawler. But the police caught them eventually and they were sent back to England.

So I didn't fall for this Canada farm business and they took me aside and asked me why. I told them this story, and added, "What's more, I'm going to tell it to all the lads outside."

"You'll find yourself in serious trouble if you do. Those are serious threats."

"Can you prove it?" I said, "Cos' I can bring you the bloke who can."

"Oh, him," they said, "he's a criminal, it's just as though he skipped jail."

"You've hit the nail on the head there!"

I did eventually get caught up in a couple of schemes, but they didn't take me out of England. They were work schemes and the first one was for the Government. It entailed living in a logging camp in the Lake District in one of four big huts, each holding about 150 men. You slept on rough boards with a couple of blankets and a bit of old sacking filled with straw for a pillow. Plenty of food, but not always edible.

The place, at the foot of Windermere, was called Gummers Howe, and our job was to clear all the logs off the fellside. It was hard work, particularly for people who'd never done it before. We worked every daylight hour except Sunday, when we spent the morning on camp-tidying duties and then were off duty till 6am Monday. We were supposed to get the 17 shillings and sixpence a week dole for this but all we got was one shilling a week spending money. It didn't buy much – a few cigarettes for the smokers and a few sweets for me.

There were a lot of these camps, some of them in Scotland, and several in Yorkshire, one of which involved draining a bog. But in our Lake District area it was nearly all lumber clearing, to make way for farms. We had no machinery. We would saw down a tree, lop off its branches, then drag it to the lake down a runway we'd made, then tie it together with a lot more logs and pull it to the other end of the lake for loading on to lorries. Getting the stumps out was the worst, digging all round, sawing and chopping at the roots and then using a sort of block and tackle with 30 of us heaving on the end of a rope. Sheer hard graft.

But it only lasted a week or two because there was trouble. They had all these men who didn't want to do the job in the first place; in the second place couldn't really do it, because they weren't physically fit enough; and thirdly, didn't care what happened because they had nothing to lose. They had hoped to make a bit of money to send home but when they found there wasn't even the dole, they just gave up bothering. The supervisors had quite a job to get any tasks completed.

But it was the supervisors themselves who really put

the kibosh on it. They were really tough types, like ex-sergeant-majors out of the regular army. It got about that they'd been bashing some of the chaps, holding their heads under water, getting them behind the huts and giving them a good thumping where it didn't leave marks. Then their morals came into question. Word got back to the authorities that they had been messing about with some of the young lads. So the camp was closed.

It was a beautiful scheme – and all for a shilling a week! I think it was supposed to be a cure for idle layabouts more than anything.

Twelve or 18 months later, during another spell of unemployment, I had my dole stopped and was back on the Means Test. This time they sent me to a farm in Yorkshire, on the moors just outside Bradford. I had my head screwed on right this time: I was going to be paid my dole, sent to me by post each week. I'd even walked most of the way there to save money. They'd given me a travel voucher and I'd managed to cash part of it in at the railway station. Walking from Stalybridge was no bother.

I arrived a day or so late. The farmer was a typically wizened Yorkshire hill farmer: "Where've you been?"

"Well, I've had to walk it."

"Didn't you get a voucher?"

"Yes, but I lost it."

"You gambled it, you mean."

"I don't gamble, I don't play cards."

"Well I've lost two days from you, so you'll 'ave to pull it up some way or t'other."

I thought, here we go.

"Where're you going to sleep?" he said.

"I don't know, I haven't had a look round yet; where would you suggest?"

"You can sleep in the barn but it'll cost you fifteen shillings a week."

"But I only get seventeen and six."

"That's nowt to do wi' me. You can sleep in't barn, no smoking, no lights, no matches, and it's fifteen bob a week."

"What about food?"

"You provide your own," he said. "I can't afford to feed you for only fifteen bob a week."

"That only leaves me with half a crown to get food for the week!"

"That's nowt to do wi' me, lad."

"Have you had many blokes here then?"

"A few."

"Well you'd better start looking for somebody else, because I'm not stopping."

I turned round and set off on the long trek back home.

And there he stood, him and his missus, shouting after me, "We'll sue you! We've been two weeks without any 'elpers. We'll 'ave you in court!" Incredible – but you didn't think about it that way. You were just bitter. I could cheerfully have beaten his skull in.

To keep up morale at this time, some of the unemployed had got themselves organised. One bunch of unemployed musicians, for instance, built up a brass band. They'd play on parades and in parks along with the regular bands and put some of the money raised into buying uniforms. Another crowd started a football league: the Wednesday 9.45am queue would play the 3.15pm queue. Whatever queue could raise a football team could join the league, playing on crofts or in public parks.

Then there were the advice bureaux, usually run by

one or two chaps who had enough knowledge of all the rules and regulations, the officials' twisted little plans. The bureau would be in somebody's front parlour, and you could go and see them if you had a grievance or were due before a tribunal. One of them would go along as an advocate and make sure everything was run as legally as it was supposed to be.

So they were getting a bit organised, and when one of these silly little bits of nonsense came up, to get you doing a lot of work for nothing, the bureau more or less nipped it in the bud. They did a lot of good. But for me, and for thousands like me, it was too little, too late.

ON THE ROAD

CHAPTER 7

FIFTY THOUSAND DOSSERS

AFTER the row with the Means Test inspector, I had to leave home. I couldn't stay and not be bringing in any money, so I took off. And tens of thousands did the same, roaming the country, ostensibly looking for work, but really just too ashamed to rely on their parents or families.

Dossers, they called them, to distinguish them from dyed-in-the-wool tramps, for whom it was a way of life. Most of them were from the cities, with no idea how to survive in the country. They weren't even fit enough, or well-equipped enough, for regular long stints of walking, but they had to tramp round the country, and a lot died of exposure and starvation. We called it famished, starved to death, hungry, died of hunger. But then they coined a new word, malnutrition, and when they put it in the papers it didn't sound as bad. The bloke was just as dead, but it sounded more acceptable; similar to today, with the word hypothermia replacing poverty. They don't say someone died of poverty, they say they died of hypothermia. Basically it means they hadn't enough money to keep warm, but it sounds better.

Anyway, there were hundreds of people, mainly dossers who didn't know their way about, who died by the wayside, beside haystacks and in barns, seeking shelter. I don't think the coroners really bothered. An inquest was only a formality. I came across quite a few bodies, in ditches and behind hedges. One was once brought into a lodging house where I was staying. They laid him out on the breakfast table. A bit grim it was.

And the charitable organisations were of little use once you were on the road. We still have a relic of it today: you can't get social security money if you have no fixed place of residence. But then it was even worse. The dole was the only place you could get money and you were on the road because that had been stopped. Even if you had a fixed abode it was like breaking into the Bank of England getting anything out of the Board of Guardians, or NAB as it became.

As for charitable organisations, if you were a tramp you might as well save your breath. You approached churches and parsons for anything. Even to the poor you didn't exist. You had nowhere to turn. There were special workhouse wards in the hospitals. They'd take you there after a serious accident or if you were incapacitated. But the common theory among the tramping fraternity was that the workhouse wards were staffed by butchers!

Anyway, I took to the road. But unlike most of the dossers' army, I was more or less equipped for it. I'll come to that later. For now, I'd better spend a bit of time distinguishing between the dosser and the tramp.

In the case of tramps, they had chosen the life out of preference, but the law called them vagrants and used the Vagrancy Act against them. This made it a crime to be without money. You could be taken before a magistrate for 'wandering abroad without visible means of subsistence'. To be destitute was a crime; it still is – the law remains to this day.

Dossers like me, on the other hand, were on the road

because of the Means Test; partly to look for work. We knew there was none to be got, but hoped we would at least find something to keep us going for a week or two. But in reality we didn't want to be a burden on our families; without us they could get no more money, but at least they would not have us to keep.

Everybody hoped the recession would not last for ever, but it took years for stability to return. It didn't help that the normal tramp population had already been considerably increased by the demobilisation after the First World War. Those who survived had been promised by Government and Press (while the bands were playing and the flags were flying) that when they returned they would have homes 'fit for heroes'.

But after the bands had gone home to polish their bugles, and the flags had been taken down to make tablecloths, a lot of the chaps found they had no homes to go to, for one reason or another, and no jobs either. Employers weren't prepared to sack people who'd been working for four and a half years just to take a soldier back on. In any case, most soldiers, while learning to kill, had missed out on developments and technical changes in their jobs. So thousands lost their jobs and with them their hopes and many of them took to the road. Eventually they formed a nucleus of a few hundred traditional type tramps, not entirely happy with it, but at least surviving, and preferable to going back to unskilled factory work.

Then came the massive new influx in my day – the Means Test dossers. We weren't a few hundred. We probably numbered tens of thousands, I don't know, but I would put it between fifty and a hundred thousand of us, roaming the country. Mostly it was single men like myself, but married men also took off, out over the moors. The tragedy was that they weren't prepared for it. The average chap who had worked all his life in a factory didn't know how to stay alive if he couldn't find food. And with all these thousands roaming the country, begging, trying to find an odd job to get a shilling or two, there just wasn't enough food to go round.

Mind you, I'm not denying that a lot of trouble was fostered by the dossers themselves. The worst of them, being townies and with no conception of country life, antagonised the farmers from the start, nipping through hedges and pinching spuds or swedes, whatever they could get. Or the damned fools would creep into barns at night and light candles. One spark in a barn full of hay and the whole lot goes up. It happened often, so farmers began to keep dogs in their barns to stop it.

If only the dossers had gone to the farm and asked, they might have been given a meal and an old outhouse to shelter in. But not after the first six or twelve months. By then we were all under suspicion, dossers and tramps alike. It only wants one or two bad apples and the whole barrel is condemned.

Actually it is possible to survive in the country, and I was lucky: I knew my way about. I could snickle a rabbit and tickle a trout; tips picked up from an old poacher in Nelson when I was very young. And I knew what greens I could pick up off the hedge backings, what sort of stuff would cook up into reasonable food to keep me alive.

Once you've caught a rabbit, it's reasonably easy to make a stew of it without any stealing. There are all sorts of edible leaves: dock, dandelion, sorrel and hawthorn. You could practically live on hawthorn leaves. We used to eat them when we were kids. We called them bread and cheese. The cellulose in all these leaves is not extensive and they can be softened into an edible sort of stew. Not particularly tasty, but it will keep you alive.

I learned one or two other tricks from the old time tramps. Smoking for instance. I got going on beech leaves. One tramp showed me the trick of breaking off a couple of twigs with plenty of leaves on, hanging them from my rucksack and walking all day till the sun dried them. No nicotine in it, but at least it tastes like smoking tobacco. Only trouble is, it's powdery and a pipeful is soon gone. Another chap I met smoked raspberry leaves – a smokeable mixture but a bit too strong for me. Others used lavender and various such flavourings. You could smoke nearly anything if it was dried properly.

Soap pills were a very efficient laxative, the old tramps' standby. They believed every ailment, every pain, every ache, all stemmed from the stomach. Oh aye, they'd say, that's your blood that's out of order, your stomach's not feeding the blood properly. Out would come the soap, and they'd cut a little piece off, about as big as a pea, and swallow it. And right or wrong, they did seem to keep in better health than most people.

In turn, I passed on a few tips of my own to the old boys. Surprisingly, for all their experiences on the road under these terrible conditions, they knew very few dodges. I showed them an old camping tip, for instance, how to make waterproof matches. You just melt the stub of a candle in a tin, then dip the matches into it. They'll never go damp and they'll always strike.

I was also lucky in that before all this started, I had managed to get a little tent, made from some scrap cloth my mother had bought for a few shillings when she worked at Dicky Howarth's mill in Salford. I'd also made a sleeping bag out of a blanket. A couple of pans from Woolworth's, a home-made rucksack, and that was it. I'd be out weekends and holidays, hiking as we called it then, rambling. We used to go out camping, up in the mountains, over the moors. I had mixed with a lot of experts on country lore, and I kept it all in mind when I got ready to go on the road.

Also I never let my appearance go. I had a tiny fold-up razor which fitted in my pocket and I always kept myself shaved. I carried a soldier's hussif – the old 'housewife', with needles and cotton and a little pair of fold-up scissors, and I could patch myself up if I got worn or torn. All in all, I managed to keep myself fairly tidy with everything in the rucksack, unlike the dosser or the tramp, who usually carried a bag. Around 1928, I even met a couple of old-style tramps carrying all their worldly goods in a spotted handkerchief on a stick, like in the cartoons.

With my home-made rucksack I looked at least halfway respectable. Of course you can't keep yourself like you did at home; you might have three pairs of socks but you've only one pair of trousers, one jacket, and a mac. I used to wash my shirt in a stream and hang it over my rucksack and let it dry in the sun as I went along. It wasn't just for comfort, it helped me to survive. I'd call at a farmhouse: "Can you find me a job to do to pay for a meal? I'll chop some wood, fodder the cows or muck the shippens out, whatever you want." And lots of people would help you. They didn't really want the jobs doing but they'd do it because you looked reasonable and you spoke reasonably. There were a lot of bad 'uns that would set the dog on you, but I made friends too; people I was to go back and visit many years afterwards.

Not long ago, someone asked me: "Where did you make for when you started out each day?" Well, it is a tramp's superstition or tradition, that if you try to make for somewhere, you'll never get there. So although he might make a short journey to meet somebody or to hit a crop for a few days' work, he never planned it long term, to arrive at a certain place. And that was how I did it too. I used to come out of my tent, my spike, or wherever I happened to be, without a thought in my mind. I would look up at the sky to see which way the clouds were blowing. I'd feel the wind on my face and think, well, either I'll walk with it or walk against it. I'd listen to the leaves rustling in the trees and make my mind up there and then by the signs I saw, which way I was heading. It didn't matter much if I'd just come down that way. I would go back by a slightly different route. If I'd come down from the north I would head back north, simply because I wanted the wind on my face or at my back, or because I liked the look of the fields in the distance.

It certainly didn't pay to plan too far ahead. For instance, I once met a dosser who seemed to have taken to the life and fitted in with it well. He used to walk from the south coast right up into Scotland, then turn around and go back. But Scotland had become a bad place for tramps. The police ran you out on sight. So now he regularly walked the length of England and back. His favourite place was the North East. They had a long history of being out of work and strikes and starvation, and, like Lancashire, had the reputation of helping anybody who was down. He'd make his way to Durham, Sunderland, or Newcastle, wander around for a week or two, then turn south again. If he'd come up from Southampton, he'd go back to Brighton. Then after a day or two, or a week or two, he'd head back up to the North West, to the Lakes, to Cumbria.

He was a pleasant bloke. He had once worked in an office, I think. His wife had died and when he'd lost his job and been knocked off the dole, off he'd gone. He'd had a rough time adapting to it but he was intelligent enough to see his way round things and he'd more or less grown to like it.

But he had become obsessed with this back-and-forth habit. And when I next met him, somewhere south of Nottingham, he'd had an enforced rest because of a wrenched ankle. The council had given him a bit of money to rest up in a lodging house until he was better. Trouble was, he was making himself ill, fretting because he couldn't go south. He was becoming tied to it – always a bad thing. You didn't dare get tied to anything. You'd look at the sky and decide to go where the clouds were going, or the opposite way, and leave it at that. Because wherever you arrived that night, you'd be going somewhere else in the morning, and this is what you had to get used to.

CHAPTER 8

THE SPIKE

Paul loved city images (photograph Paul Graney).

AS I HAVE said, it wasn't too bad for me. If I couldn't get under a proper roof for the night, I could always pitch my little tent somewhere out in the fields, or on the moors. I've even pitched it by the roadside and had the police come knocking on the front flap. Who was I? Where was

I going? Because I always managed to keep myself decent, the coppers usually more or less turned a blind eye. But where did the rest of the dossers go for the night? Where did I head for, for that matter, if civilisation was within reach or the weather was particularly bad? To the casual ward in the workhouse, that's where. Tramps called it the Spike. I've never been able to find out why. The traditional tramp would head for one only if the weather was bad.

Provided there was room and you had no money, admission to a spike was free. Every town that had a workhouse had a casual ward attached and they made their own times for opening, usually between 5pm and 6pm. You were not allowed to queue at the door. When you were approaching one, you would see a chap in a doorway, another one or two down a side street, all hiding, but within sight of the door. As soon as it opened they would make a dash. That's if there were a lot. And by the time we Means Test dossers got on the road, there were a lot. A hell of a lot. So it was a matter of strategic importance to find yourself a hiding place, from which the police wouldn't move you on, yet within sight of the spike doorway. It did wonders for your self-respect, did that.

If you got in, first thing you did was sign the book. You'd been on the road, you had nothing, no home. But you had to turn out your pockets and if you had sixpence, they turned you out and said you should go to the doss house, even if the nearest was three four or more miles away. The point was that in some of the very cheap dosses you could get a bed for fourpence. They were officially entitled Model Lodging Houses!

At the spike, after asking your name, they also wanted your address. Here you were, on the road, sleeping under hedges and in barns, and they were asking for your address! I questioned this once. I said, "What sort of address are you expecting?" He said, "Well, it's in the rules! I have to ask for it."

Once you had made something up and got past the Gestapo on the counter, it was bathtime. There were various kinds, but usually a sort of slipper bath, about six inches of luke-warm water, contained behind a twelve-inch tiled wall. You'd have 15 or 16 men standing in this, trying to soap themselves down, then all trying to rinse themselves with the same dirty water. You were not allowed to let the water go and run some clean, so the lice and dirt were just sort of redistributed.

After that ordeal, in some larger town spikes, you would be deloused, either with a spray of liquid or a generous puff of Keating's powder, in your hair and all over your body. You weren't allowed to wash it off, you had to put your clothes back on over it. If there was a delousing station, there was no way to dodge it. It was compulsory.

Actually, rolling in bracken is just as effective. Over the years, several old-time traditional tramps gave me this tip. You could only do it when the bracken was about, but it was a really good louse and flea shifter. Get a couple of handfuls of bracken leaves, powder them up and rub yourself all over with it. It won't kill them, but they won't stay on you.

But it didn't matter in the spike, however clean you had kept yourself. If the delousing man was there, that was that. I don't know whether it was the Keating's that did it, but some chaps used to come out in a terrible rash. If they heard the delouser was in action, they didn't dare go in the place.

After that, it was teatime. The food varied

tremendously. In the north it was more common to get a good meal than a bad one. In the Midlands they were really mean – you might get just one round of bread and cheese. You've heard the saying, as thick as a workhouse butty. Well, a workhouse butty in some of these places was about an inch and a half thick and was known as 'bread and scrape', the scrape being a thin film of margarine and a thin paring of cheese, cut so fine you could see through it if you held it up to the light – hardly enough to taste. In other places, after a long day on the road, remember, tea would be a round of bread and jam and a mug of very weak tea. It looked like last night's tea brewed again. Made me glad I stuck to water.

Yet I remember once being in a little village in Yorkshire, where the workhouse master's wife did the catering. She came into this casual ward where we were all sitting in front of the fire, 15 or 16 of us. "Well lads," she said. "Are you all hungry? What would you like for your tea?" And she rhymed off half a dozen things. We ended up having real northern potato pie, made in a deep enamel dish topped with a thick crust. One of the best pies I've ever tasted.

On the other hand, as I said, you could just have a couple of thick rounds of bread chucked at you, plus a surly look. Same in the morning. A bit of bacon and fried bread if you were very lucky, or more usually the old bread and margarine and a mug of tea.

At many spikes, more than there should have been, the workhouse masters (or the casual ward minders) seemed to think your presence was an imposition. The authorities had set them up for the very purpose of feeding the road men, but they treated us like dirt, as though they had to punish us for some sort of offence.

When I said earlier that accommodation in the spike was free, don't get me wrong. You had to work to pay for your night's lodging and, depending on the spike concerned, this could lead to quite a tragedy.

Every place had different jobs to be done. Some of it was normal cleaning, but I have cleaned the hospital wards of bedridden old people, scrubbed stone corridors, climbed on roofs and helped re-slate them, dug drain channels for plumbers. Anything there was to do, the casual ward did it. At Glossop spike, I worked on their big farm, breaking stones for its roads. You could be there till midday or later and this is where the tragedy comes in. You were not allowed to stay at a spike for more than one night. You had to move on and the next spike might be 16 miles away, sometimes more than 20 if you were out in the rural districts.

So if you wanted to get into a spike by that night, you had to cover that distance between, say, 12.30pm and 5pm, which was manifestly impossible. So you had to beg, or make money somehow, to pay for a doss house bed, or face the prospect of sleeping rough. I've slept in railway carriages parked in railway sidings and in covered railway wagons. I've slept in parked farm lorry cabs, which was possible then because they didn't lock them like they do now.

As long as you were away early in the morning you were all right, and you were out of the weather. I only tended to do this when the temperature was below zero. Otherwise, I'd put up my tent and could stay warm no matter where I was.

It wasn't so easy for others, the unprepared city blokes. They must have died in their hundreds. I wrote letters about it, years afterwards when I was back home, to various people: MPs, health authorities and parish councils.

Three or four years later the rule was altered. Men were to be given sufficient time to get to the next place of shelter, and if they had 20 miles to go they had to be given a full day to do it in. Perhaps my little bit of protest helped.

One thing I ought to have mentioned about the cheap doss houses, was the rope. One or two still existed at that time and I had heard about them from old-timers. If you didn't have fourpence for a bed, you could sleep 'on the rope'. This was a fairly thick rope, suspended from two hooks across the clear space at the end of a dormitory. For tuppence you could hang your arms over this rope and, with a bit of luck, you would spend some of the night asleep. I believe that in Glasgow, right up to the war, it was still going. It was known there as the 'penny lean'.

CHAPTER 9

TALES OVER THE TABLE

IN THE spikes and a lot of the doss houses, there were no home comforts, and after you'd had your meal there was nothing to do. In the workhouse spike you weren't allowed out. In a doss house you had freedom up to around 10pm and then you all had to be in. You couldn't sit comfortably, though there was usually a common room where you did everything except sleep.

There were long tables and crude benches, both usually homemade. You had your meals on these tables and when you'd finished, whoever was duty man would clear them. If there was any socialising to be done, you usually stayed sitting at the table. If it was cold and there was a fire you'd take the benches and sit round it, otherwise, groups would gather near the radiators.

It was not often that anyone wanted to talk, however. They were a fairly close-mouthed lot, living silent lives. They might spend a week without speaking to anybody. That applied to me, too. More than once, I've gone a week or more just talking to trees and squirrels, to make sure my voice was still working.

As for my companions, if they did want to talk, they'd usually do it across the table, more often than not just passing on news. A lot of the old-timers were not very articulate so they'd restrict it to news of who they'd seen and where, and messages from one to the other. And they certainly knew how to keep it short. "Old Jumping Jimmy wants his drum back," told the bloke receiving the message that Jimmy, wherever he now was, had not forgotten that the bloke had pinched his brew can and still intended to get it back. Or Bacon Jack might have passed a message on. It might be a fairly long one, but when it reached its target it might have been reduced to: "Bacon Jack wants to see thee." And that was it. It was no good asking "Where?", because this thing might have been six months in transmission and Bacon Jack might be at the other end of the country.

They would bump into each other eventually. If either of them heard that the other was in a range of 50 miles or so and wanted to pass another message on, they would put it on the 'drums'. That's what they called this underground telegraph, after the African signalling drums I suppose. And it worked; the messages circulated all round England. I listened to them a lot, and now and again they would spark someone into reminiscence and it really was worth listening to these old timers and their experiences, often going back to the 1880s, on the rare occasions that they would open up and talk about them. I've tried to remember one or two.

Like Stoker. He was turned 60 when I met him, a chap with a fair amount of intelligence. Not so much formal education; he was a bit like me, left school when he was very young. But in addition to the normal intelligence of the countryside, which most of these chaps had, he'd spent quite a lot of time in libraries sheltering from the cold. He had not only read quite a lot, but assimilated it too, something I never achieved, to any great extent. We were more or less kindred spirits, because we shared this little spark of education. We never 'roaded' it, we never 'pounded it' together, but we enjoyed quite a few chats across the table.

Stoker met his end when he was killed by a runaway horse. Some people say he was trying to stop it, but I don't think so. I don't like to denigrate the dead, but I think it was more likely that he was panic-stricken and ran across the road trying to get out of the way.

Anyway, I once asked him how he got the name Stoker. I thought he must have been in the Navy because quite a few naval terms had drifted into civilian life. I knew two Tiffies, which is from the Navy 'artificer', or mechanic, who were still called that long after the war. But Stoker said that wasn't the reason.

"No," he said, "it came about when I lived just outside Hereford. We were a bit wild and we'd gone into Hereford one night, me and another bloke and we'd got tiddly and missed the last bus, such as it was, and we were too drunk to walk, so we got into the railway siding intending to sleep it off in a railway carriage. Then we found an engine that still had steam up. My mate said, 'I can drive one of these, let's go back on it.' So we drove it back, about eight or ten miles."

Of course it wasn't long before the police latched on to who'd done it, because they had stopped it so near to where they lived and left it there, on the line. They ended up in court, and apparently all my friend could say in his defence was, "Well, it wasn't really me, I were only t'stoker. I only shovelled t'coal in." It became his nickname and followed him all his life. I never knew his real name. On the road you never asked a man for that.

Most of the old timers had nicknames, but this is something the dossers never copied. They were leading the same life as the genuine tramps, walking the roads trying to get by, but they didn't enjoy it and it showed. So they never acquired the same reputation, or the nicknames. There was old Fo'penny Aggie, for instance. I kept hearing about her because there were few women on the road back then. I came across one or two, but never to speak to. Her name intrigued me. I kept asking, "Who is Fo'penny Aggie? And why's she called Fo'penny Aggie?"

"Oh, you'll know when you meet her, lad."

Then one day I was with a bloke in Lincolnshire whose name, like many, I never knew. We were heading towards Retford, when he said, "There's one of our lot somewhere near here … I can smell smoke." We sniffed our way to the fire, and there was Fo'penny Aggie, just getting her drum of tea going. We sat with her and she gave my mate a cup of tea, whilst I stuck my head in the stream and got a drink of water. I never drank tea, still don't.

She was small, no more than eight stone and very soft-spoken, a well-educated voice, with just a hint of the West Country burr. She was as ragged as the rest of us, with a face like an old boot, all beaten up with the weather. But she spoke very nicely, did Fo'penny Aggie. I liked her.

"Why is she called that?" I asked, as we walked away down the road.

"Well," he says, "if we'd got on to the subject of coppers, she would have told you. She thinks that policemen are the worst creatures that ever crawled on God's earth. She will whip out her purse and show you fourpence, and tell you: 'While I've got that, nobody can run me in, because that's enough to find a night's bed.'"

It appears that Aggie had had quite a few run-ins with the police. One of the most famous started when she was passing through a well-to-do suburb, and she saw a bloke deliberately kicking a dog to death. She ran into the garden, picked up a piece of fence post and beat this fellow over the head with it and split his skull open, laid him out on the ground. She always used to swear that the dog had then died in her arms.

In the meantime the bloke's wife had rung the police, but when one arrived, Aggie set about him with the fence post as well. He backed out into the street, whilst she stood in the garden brandishing the post, defying him to come and get her. The wife rang the police station again and four more coppers came, making five altogether. She looked like she couldn't lift a matchbox off the table, but it took five of them all their time to run her in.

Nobody ever knew the outcome, whether she got a sentence or not. One story said that they stuck her in a cell overnight, and when she'd cooled down they sent her on her way because of what the bloke had done to the dog. You've got to be a character when the men of the road talk about you like that. You've got to have something special.

One of the oddest characters was Mad Halifax; a strange bloke, muttering to himself all the time and always the same theme. He must have had some bad experience in Halifax, but nobody ever got it out of him what had happened. But all the time, he would be muttering. I only ever saw him once but I believe he was like that all the time. The only time he stopped was to eat. But as soon as the meal was over he would restart his diatribe: "Halifax! I'd drown the lot of them! Halifax! They're all mad in Halifax!" He'd go on all night and people used to go to bed to get out of his way. You couldn't stop him. On and on. Each rant lasted about ten minutes, then he would go back to the beginning again. He wasn't popular!

Chalky was a quiet enough fellow, but his particular

obsession was the gypsies' code that told what the people in a house were like. Sometimes they'd leave a couple of little pebbles and a small stick outside it, quite inconspicuous. You'd walk straight past and never guess that they meant: these people are good, you can get a meal here. Or other codes: these people will buy your pegs or whatever you're selling; if you're a tinker, they will let you have anything they've got to mend; these people are not so good, but may be talked into it; these will call the police; these have a dog running loose.

I used to know a good few of these signs but I've long since forgotten them. Often, they were in chalk rather than sticks and pebbles, and these were what Chalky specialised in. Basically, he was a beggar. He'd knock on a door and say he was trying to get to see his mother who was very ill and he had no money and he had to walk it, could they help him with a few coppers, a meal, anything – just plain begging. He would only knock when he felt the old fellow was out at work.

But everywhere he called, he carefully chalked his signals outside. The job wasn't complete if he didn't. Like I say, an obsession. So you can imagine what he was like the night I met him in a spike and he'd run out of chalk. He was really upset. He came to me and said, "I know you've got pencil and paper, Paul, but you don't have any chalk, do you?" I said, "No, I never use it, Chalky."

He was really downcast, so in the morning when we came out of the spike, I said, "Come with me, Chalky." I had a few shillings in my pocket, which I'd carefully hidden from the warden, and we went to a little newsagents where I paid a penny for a packet of five pieces of school chalk. He was set up – I thought he was going to lick my boots! He'd never had that much chalk in one go before.

I never ran into him again but he must have talked about it, because I kept getting repercussions. Someone over the table would say, "Chalky's still talking about you, Paul." That's the way it was. Very few people told bad stories about each other. There were crooks and bad hats amongst them, but you didn't talk about them. You'd probably get your clock knocked round if you did.

Nicknames – I'm remembering a few more that I jotted down at the time. Often I didn't know the men themselves, but I'd hear their names in conversation. For instance Bowdy. I don't know whether that was his real name, but his nickname was Cowboy. He never moved out of Yorkshire and I had the pleasure of walking with him one day and he spent hours telling me tales about Horsehair Jack and Stuttering Ginger, Mushroom Tom, Shackles Punch and Tinwhistle Joe.

"How did you get the name Cowboy?" I asked. I kept mentioning America because I thought he must have been there. Then I shut up because he kept avoiding the issue and I thought he had something to hide. But suddenly he said, "Look, if you want to know, lad, I'll tell you. It's many years ago, before the First War. I was in Skipton. I'd been doing a bit of farm work," he said, "and when I got paid I'd gone in the boozer, and got a load on. I wanted to get to Leeds where I had better chance of a lift on a wagon. So I thought I'd get a lift towards it on a canal boat. Very often an extra body on a boat didn't matter and a lot of the bargees had a soft spot for me. They'd pull into the bank, and say, 'Jump on,' and I might even get a meal out of the bargee's missus.

"So I got on the cut bank and started walking. I was

in a right state ... you know what these Taddy ales are like! Anyway, along came a boat and I called to the boatman: 'What's the chance of a ride to Leeds?' He pulled the boat up and said: 'It's dinnertime, come and have a meal first.' Well, they gave me a meal and the boatman said, 'You want to get to Leeds, do you? I'll tell you what, you can be the engineer if you like. I haven't got an engineer.' 'What do I do for that?' I said. 'Tha' leads th'orse,' he replied.

"Well! I was so fuddled it never clicked. I walked all the way from Skipton to Leeds holding that horse's head and I didn't realise till we got near Leeds and I was dead beat, what I'd done. Anyway, he gave me a couple of bob and had a good laugh. And ever since then I've been called Cowboy."

I met a good few characters like Cowboy, though there weren't so many left when I was roading it. These were the chaps who'd been doing it in 1870, 1880 – on the road since they were kids. They'd some howler stories to tell. I only wish I'd had a tape recorder in those days. I did make quite a few notes, but they were lost over the years.

One chap had been a lion tamer, a conjuror, a thought reader, every job there was, in and around circuses. He showed me some battered old newspaper cuttings of himself. Then he'd had an accident, got run over and trapped by a wagon. He was partly crippled and he'd ended up on the road. He couldn't stay still, couldn't live in a house.

There were lots more. Over my years on the road I generated a tremendous respect for most of them.

But the dossers were different. They were men without a tradition. Some were decent chaps with good stories, good backgrounds. They fitted in, they survived, but many were disgruntled and bitter and should never have been in that position. They couldn't make a go of it, and for many of them the penalty was to die under a hedge somewhere.

CHAPTER 10

CONGER AND TINWHISTLE

YOU WOULD usually be alone when you set off in the morning. Men did not often team up together. Occasionally, if they happened to be going the same way, and had known each other for years, they might walk a day, or part of a day, together.

But if you're begging, if you're on the bum, or if you're looking for a bit of a job to get yourself a few shillings, you can't do it if there's two of you. Two can't go on the knocker, so it is essentially a lonely sort of existence. Men got used to being silent. It had to be something important before they would talk at any length, and many became more or less inarticulate. Nights could be as miserable as sin, and you really needed the rare outgoing type, such as Conger, to liven things up.

Conger Eel had been a sailor. He was shortish and fat. On the road and he was fat! It must have been glandular. He also had a wooden leg, an old-fashioned wooden stump. He'd been in the Royal Navy and later in the Merchant Navy. And he was a real extrovert. He would come into a room with all of us sitting there, wet through, steaming, trying to dry out our clothes round a radiator, nobody speaking, everybody drooping and wishing it was summer again. And in he'd bounce: "God bless all of yer. Including them as I don't like and them as doesn't like me!"

People would immediately perk up; grins on faces

that never smiled, and on he'd chatter, all the time we were eating, often about his amorous conquests. How he made any of these was a mystery, because he certainly wasn't glamorous or well-dressed. He was clean enough, like a lot of the old time tramps, but in an era of short back and sides, the long hair curling around his collar marked him out for what he was.

I had to ask him eventually – nicknames have always fascinated me – how he came to be called Conger. "Oh," he said, "it's a long story, that."

"Well, I said, we've got all night, go on."

So he told me how he'd once been shipwrecked. The ship had caught fire, and because they had more than enough lifeboats, he had ended up alone in one. "There was no danger," he said. "It was calm, the lifeboat was equipped with food and water for several people and we were in the shipping lanes, so I wasn't worried.

"But there was a swordfish circling around the boat and something must have annoyed it because it attacked and made a hole in the bottom of the boat. It started to sink and you can't afford to be in the water with sharks around, so I put my foot through the hole to try and stop it from sinking while I baled. I had my foot through that hole for a day and a night and it had gone shrivelled and dead-white like a piece of tripe, when a damned great conger eel came and bit it off. Luckily I was picked up the day after. I'd used a tourniquet to stop the bleeding, and later they took my leg off up to the knee. And here I am."

All right, I know, it's an incredible story, but I don't think chaps like Conger had the will to tell you a fairy tale just for the fun of it. Maybe failing memory distorted what they told you, but I'm sure they believed they were telling the truth.

I don't know what to think about Conger. He was certainly an amazing chap and I'll never forget his favourite story. I heard it once or twice. If there were new faces at the table, usually at mealtimes, he would also tell about when he fought the octopus. He said he'd been diving for pearls off the Great Barrier Reef. This I believed, because a lot of sailors, particularly merchantmen, would skip ship to look for money like that. He said they would use a sort of bucket over their heads, a primitive diving helmet that held another couple of breaths, a pocket of air that allowed them to stay down a minute or so longer.

"There I were, down on t'bottom," he said, "filling my basket with these oyster shells, and I felt a tap on my shoulder. Now bottom of t'sea is no place to feel a tap on your shoulder. So I swung round and there was this octopus, staring at me. Well, what do you do with an octopus at t'bottom o' t'sea. It's got eight legs to start with, all full of suckers. And then it wrapped one of its legs round my arm and tried to pull me towards it."

He would then go off into a vivid description of his battle under the sea and losing all his air, and how eventually he struggled to the surface and the blokes on the boat pulled him in. "And you know, he said, it was still clinging to my arm. They'd a hell of a job to pry it loose. It was a good fifteen inches across!" Which usually raised a gale of laughter, or at least a few grins. By hell, we needed some laughter too! It took a lot to make these fellows smile. There were one of two blokes who could make very witty remarks and raise a laugh here and there, and people like Conger with his fund of stories, but entertainment like this was very rare.

After Conger, you might go three or four months

before seeing anyone who could put on a bit of a show. So someone like Tinwhistle Joe was another godsend. It was surprising the tunes requested by the dossers, the unwilling tramps. Always something to remind them of home and always morbidly sentimental. First World War songs such as 'Keep the Home Fires Burning' were the favourites. Of course, we weren't long out of the war. He used to play quite a few songs and tunes from that period, sitting amongst us, his whistle cocked at an angle.

I was once about six miles out of Derby, when he came out of a field. I think he'd been knocking off a couple of turnips. He asked me where I was going, and I told him, "Through Derby and on to Nottingham."

"You won't make Nottingham tonight," he said. "I know a good doss in Derby. Stay there tonight, and I'll make you some money tomorrow. It's market day."

"Okay," I said.

"It's not legal, like."

By then I had learned the proper responses, and said, "Well, never mind the legality, is it risky?"

"Oh aye," he said. "You might get a copper on your neck but you have to risk something to get some money."

So we went to the doss and at about 10am set out to the market. There was a cheapjack there, doing a sort of Dutch auction: "Who'll give me three shillings for this? Well give me half a crown! I'll not take less than two bob." You know the type of fellow. He knew Tinwhistle Joe, and said, "Here you are, I'll start you off, Joe, get cracking," and put a shilling in Joe's cap. It was good for the stallholder, because Joe was a damned good tin whistler and people would be attracted by the sound and stay to look at the merchandise. So Joe hands the cap to me and says, "Right, Paul, you go round with this."

And the stallholder played fair by us. He'd say, "Here you are missus, you want threepence change, put it in this bloke's cap." And a lot of people did, they threw their odd coppers into the cap. "Stick the cap under their noses," says Joe. "Don't ask for owt, don't say nowt, just stick the cap under their noses, they'll cough up." And a lot of them did.

We must have got somewhere near a pound, when a copper arrived. Knowing the ropes, we split, and the copper chased after Joe. I'd stashed my rucksack outside town and I picked it up and went back to the dosshouse looking for Joe, but he'd skipped town, so I did the same.

Eight or nine months later I was a lot further south, somewhere in Gloucestershire, when someone came into the spike and said, "Tinwhistle Joe's looking for thee. He says you ran off with a lot of his money."

"I didn't run off, the coppers came. I'm waiting to catch up with him. I owe him about ten bob."

"Aye, he's been asking where you were a good while."

A couple of months later, another bloke said he'd seen Joe two or three weeks back, heading for the gypsy horse fair at Appleby, in Cumbria.

I'd no chance of walking to Appleby from Gloucestershire in time, but I finally managed to get a lift up toward Ilkley on a potato lorry, and eventually I latched on to Joe and returned his money. That's how it was. If he'd owed it to me he wouldn't have looked for me but he'd have had it for me when I'd met him. Same with the other blokes: if they owed you anything, they would go hungry before they'd spend it. It was part of the tradition. They were a lot more honest than many businessmen or so-called civilised people I've met since.

CHAPTER 11

TENTS AND OLD TIMERS

MY LITTLE tent was only about three feet high and six feet long – just shelter from the rain. When I went in a spike or a doss house, I used to stash it somewhere outside. Occasionally, if I had been working somewhere and had tuppence to spare, I would leave it in a left-luggage office. Usually, though, I'd hide it outside the town in a field. They wouldn't let me in a spike with it, and in a doss house I'd have had to tie it to my body, because they didn't only have old-timers in the doss houses, there were a lot of rogues and thieves there too, especially in the towns, because a lot of local layabouts and rough characters used them. They were always on the look-out for somebody who might have a copper or two and they would knock you on the head for a shilling.

I remember one really rough doss in Buckinghamshire on the Great North Road. It had been a warehouse or a mill and had vast, unheated rooms and mill-type windows with lots of little square panes, most of them broken. There were about 50 or 60 beds in each room, so many that you couldn't walk between them. You came in at the door and had to start clambering over the beds to get to an empty one. That doss was well avoided, but if you were in the area it was Hobson's choice.

The doss houses were a last resort really, partly because of the cost, and partly the discomfort. Spikes were not very popular either, but they were essential in bad weather. You couldn't sleep in a barn or a railway coach when the temperature was below zero. If it had been a wet day you needed somewhere to dry out. I've been in spikes where it's been like a market stall around the radiators, wet clothes galore spread out on the floor, steaming away, in an effort to get them dry by morning.

In some more enlightened spikes, they did have a sort of primitive drying room with a radiator in it, fairly warm, with a lot of nails knocked into the walls. You could hang your clothes on these and hope they would reach a sort of warm dampness by morning.

When I had to use a doss house, particularly a known rough one, I would leave everything outside ... hide my rucksack out in the fields, along with any money, except for about sixpence, then walk into town, find the doss house, pay my fee, and get into bed by nine at the latest. The more sleep I got, the fitter I was for when I cleared out in the morning to pick up my tent.

I know I got talked about because of my tent. They'd never seen anything like it and a lot of them talked about getting one. But I don't think you could buy them then, small cheap tents. As I've already said, mine was home-made. I'd been camping a long time. I also had an old army ground sheet. You could buy a damaged one at the ex-Army stores for a shilling. It was heavy, a big rubber sheet, six feet by three feet, minus a triangular piece, that made it suitable for a cape. It kept you reasonably dry and made a good ground sheet.

I took one bloke in with me once when we couldn't make it to the next spike. We looked in vain for a barn or somewhere to shelter. "Never mind," I said. "Let's get where there's some water." At a village shop we got a bit of bacon, a loaf and some margarine, and tea and sugar, which I never normally carried, with not drinking tea.

Then we made for a bit of open common, out of sight of the road. I got my tent out and this fellow stood goggle-eyed. "What the hell's that?" he said.

"It's a tent. It will keep you dry out of the rain."

We made a fire, cooked a meal, and he had a nice pot of tea. Then it started really teeming down. I had this ordinary blanket which buttoned-up to make a sleeping bag, but would open back out as a blanket. We had obtained some old newspapers to put under us instead of a blanket, and put the blanket over us. He was astounded at how warm and dry he stayed all night. "It's been a hobby of mine, roaming and climbing, before I took to the road," I explained.

"Well, you'll never come to any harm, mate, I wish I could get hold of something like this."

It made a tremendous impression. I don't know whether I ever got a nickname through it though, although I was accepted by the Old Timers, the Rangers, as they called themselves. Usually they just called me Paul, but often it was Mr Graney, usually from people who respected my 'education', little knowing that I'd left school when I was barely 13. I've always felt very proud of that acceptance, because they were such a worthwhile set of chaps. In fact, they deserve a section to themselves.

The Rangers, Yorkshire Rangers, Wold Rangers, were in a class of their own. Many of them were ragged, with big bushy white whiskers as often as not. But they kept themselves as clean and tidy as they could. They preserved their self-respect, and in turn were respected by ordinary people, not like the tramps of fiction.

What the Rangers had was not exactly a round, but they did follow the seasonal jobs around the countryside; cropping, they called it, helping with the potato lifting and then on to the apple and pear picking; mixing in with the gypsies, providing extra labour at the busy times. Hay making, planting, muck-spreading, they'd do anything to earn a bit of brass.

And because they were often in the same places two or three times a year, staying for a week or two, they were, as I say, well-respected. They were known. A Ranger would be going down a village street and some woman would see him from her doorway and call: "Hey up there, Jack, have you got room for a bit of pie?" And she'd come out with a smile and a big lump of apple pie and a thick sandwich or a bowl of soup, whatever was going. As a special treat she might even make bacon and eggs for him and he'd sit on the doorstep to eat it.

Oh yes, the Rangers were well-respected. The children used to run and hold their hands, chattering to them as they went up the street. If they had money they could go in the pub and be accepted there too. Or a regular would invite them in: "Come and have a pint before you move on, quench your thirst, old lad." Even the police gave them no bother, not in the small villages, anyway. In the towns of course, they were seen as cluttering the streets and local authorities would instruct the police to move them on, but in the villages they had friends. There was one old boy that I ran into a few times and had an odd chat with – Old Charlie. There was a little village down in South Yorkshire, a mining district. One time, I was told by one of the villagers during my passage through it at a much later date, Old Charlie had stayed there nearly three weeks.

An old lady lived there on her own and she'd often given him a meal and let him sleep in the shed. She had little money but he went into the woods for her, found dead wood and sawed it up into a pile of logs, enough to keep her in fuel through the winter. He had also done her garden over, rebuilt its drystone wall, whitewashed the shed and the back of the house and painted part of the kitchen with as much paint as she'd got. Then some of the people in the pub had a whip-round for more paint so he could do the outside, and one or two local blokes had buckled in and helped him.

He had stayed nearly three weeks helping that old lady, and he was accepted by the whole village. At night he'd sit on the garden wall and all the children would sit round while he told them fairy tales, keeping them amused for hours. He was buried locally when he died, and for years the children would put wild flowers on his grave. Yes, he was well liked, was Old Charlie.

It was pretty much the same wherever he went. He was a pleasant, well-spoken old chap and while his clothes were normal tramp's clothes, he was bodily clean. He had long hair, of course, and every now and again somebody would give him a haircut. He'd just had one when I met him once. "Just look at me, Paul," he said. "I'm starving to death, mate … they've cut all my hair off!"

CHAPTER 12

TALES OF MY OWN

Wet pavement and lone walker (photograph Paul Graney).

TALES OVER the table – I could have told a few of my own. I remember one time being near Wellington, Shropshire, just under the Wrekin, at the back end of the year. A chap staying in the same lodging house was a crop follower and on this particular occasion he'd been helping in the beet fields, before labouring in a sugar beet factory. He knew I had a sweet tooth, so he got me five pounds of sugar in a cloth bag.

I only had a small saucepan, small frying pan and a tin drinking mug, but I was determined not to waste the gift, so I set up camp for a day or two near the bottom of the Wrekin, found some good blackberries, picked a couple of pounds of apples in one of the huge orchards, then went into Wellington and bought a pound of flour and eight ounces of margarine.

I'd also acquired a biscuit tin and back at my camp I dug it into the hillside with a fire under it, and in that primitive little oven I made a whole pile of blackberry and apple pies. Well, I thought, I can't carry them round with me so I decided I would stay until I'd eaten them. It only took me a day or so. I couldn't leave them alone. I ate and ate, I was so sugar starved. Of course, they made me ill. I never did it again. But it was worth it.

I eventually packed up but wasn't sure whether to turn off to Shrewsbury or not. I was sitting on a bench outside a pub in the village of High Ercall, when the landlord came out and asked if I'd ever done any droving. I didn't know what he meant, and said I hadn't. "Well," he said, "do you want to have a go? I've half a dozen sheep I want to get down to Wellington Station and I can't take them myself."

"I'd probably lose them," I said.

"No, there's a dog and the shepherd lad to help you."

So I agreed and he said I could leave my knapsack at the pub and call back for it. The lad would get the sheep out of the field and all I had to do was get them into the pen at the station. Anyway this lad brings out, not half a dozen, but about 30 of the woolly monsters!

Sheep are queer, you know. I don't know a lot about them but when they get into a strange place, they don't want to know. They'll do anything to get back where they've come from. We got them out on the road, and true, we'd got the dog and we had this lad, but the whole damned issue turned round and more or less stampeded towards me to get back through the gate. I ran up the banking to get out of the way, and they're all there, bleating at the gate. Me and the lad got sticks, trying to prod them and push them and eventually the dog got behind them and once we'd got them out of sight of their own field, it wasn't so bad.

Tell the truth, it couldn't have been much worse. It was maybe two miles into Wellington, but it took us two and a half hours. By the time we got there, they had been all over the place! They were breaking through hedges and the dog was trying to fetch them out of fields and gardens. What a game! And of course, by this time there was a fair bit of traffic. Mainly horse-drawn, but the sheep didn't like it at all. They were bolting into shops, skittering among the traffic, running rings around the police who turned up. "Where are you going with this lot?"

"To the station," I said.

"Didn't you know that there's only certain hours early in the morning when you can take livestock through the street, before the shops are open?"

I could see myself doing 25 years in jail, and oh, those sheep! We eventually got them to the station, and they split up again. They were on the lines, they were on the platform, what a mess: porters were running about, shouting, and then the stationmaster came out. He didn't bother about the sheep, he came straight to me. "Are you in charge of this lot?"

I gave up. "Ring this bloke at the pub at High Ercall," I said. In the end it worked out fine. When I got back to the pub, he gave me a meal, and a couple of quid for my trouble.

Another time, I was on a farm just outside Grasmere. I'd had a fortnight's work there, muck-spreading. I'd put my tent down in the bottom field near the stream. The farmer's wife was very nice. She darned all my things, patched everywhere that wanted patching, put buttons on where they were missing and fed me up. Her husband was just a hill farmer, struggling along, but he gave me a few shillings. It wasn't a proper wage, but along with my keep and the state of his finances, I didn't do so bad.

Towards the end of it, I woke up one morning and there was another little tent by the side of me. A bloke got out, said he was from Liverpool, and asked if it was a camping ground. "No," I said, "I've been working for the farmer. You'd better see him if you want to stay."

"Oh no," he said, "I'll be moving off in a bit."

We got chatting and he was intrigued when I told him what I was doing, that I was a tramp, a dosser. He watched me cooking in my little pan and shaving and asked if he could join me for a time when I moved on. He seemed harmless enough, so I agreed, and after a week or so, we'd arrived at the Black Hills, a big wooded area between Wolverhampton and Birmingham.

We'd got a rabbit stew going with some wild garlic to flavour it, various herbs, and young dandelion leaves too, when two girls wandered into our camp. They were lost. They wanted to get to Wolverhampton. It was about 7pm. "We'll show you," we said. "We'll get you on to the road where you can get a bus … it's not far. Have something to eat with us."

So they sat down. They thought it was marvellous, this gypsy life and when we were putting them on the bus, I said we would take them out that Saturday night.

We had eightpence between us. This bloke said, "What got into you to say that? What are we going to do? Sit in the park with four twopennorths of chips?"

"No, I'll show you how to make some money."

We got into Wolverhampton on the Saturday morning. Now in any town of any size, near the market, in one of the back streets, there was usually a shop that sold hawkers' wares such as clothes pegs, at ridiculous prices. We bought six anti-splash washers, the little tubes that you fit on your tap, took three apiece and went off into the working class terraced house areas, and started knocking on doors. Within ten minutes I'd sold my three for fourpence each. I went straight back to the shop for another dozen, and there was my mate doing the same. By the end of the day, I think I'd made eight shillings and he'd made between ten and twelve, which gave us a tidy sum of money to take the girls out.

We blued the lot that Saturday night. Best seats at the pictures, with chocolates and ice cream, and a good fish and chip supper. Those girls never knew that we were both tramps, well, that I was anyway. Never saw them again.

This fellow gave me his address in Liverpool, saying, if I was ever there, to look him up. Twenty-odd years later, well after the war, I was in Liverpool and saw the name over a big ships' chandlers. On impulse I went in and asked to see the boss. "I don't think he'll know my name," I said, "but ask him if he remembers having a fish and chip supper with Paul in Wolverhampton." My hunch was right. The manager took me straight in, and my old chum jumped up. "I couldn't remember your name," he said, "but I remember those bloody fish and chips! I've never had such a good time in my life. I talk about it to this day. It was one of the best times of my life, those couple of weeks we spent tramping together."

He wanted me to come over and said he'd find me a job there, but I had a fairly good job at the time and I didn't want to uproot. I went back to see him once or twice and we corresponded. His father was a near-millionaire and he was just mooching around, camping out and latching on to climbing parties in the Lakes, didn't know what to do with himself.

I'm sorry I lost touch with some people. I was once walking near Knottingley, 'tother side of Leeds, when a car pulled up. They were pretty rare, were motor cars. The bloke and his wife asked if I wanted a lift. Was I lost? Where was I going? I said, "I don't know. I'm just walking to see where I get to, what's on the other side of the hill." This seemed to fascinate them. They said, "Well, jump in and tell us about it."

When we pulled up in Knottingley we went into a pub and they offered to buy me a big meal. "I'm not hungry, I get enough to eat," I protested.

"Well," they said, "somebody else's cooking is always better than your own."

When I told them who I was, what I was and whatnot, they couldn't get over it. They said, "We've read about this, you know, all these thousands of people like yourself who're having to tramp the roads because they've no money and don't want to be a burden on their families, but you're the first we've met. Come on home with us and stay a few days and we can have a good chat."

So I went for a couple of days, but it was a peculiar

situation. When you're out on your own and making your own way you feel straight, but when people do things like this, you feel like a charity case, although they're being nice and good in their way. And I strongly suspect that these people were using the information I gave them, either for writing or for research. They were asking clinical questions, leading questions, and I got a bit suspicious, clammed up and moved on. But I must admit, they were very hospitable.

CHAPTER 13

ONE THOUSAND DAYS OF NOTHING

IT SOUNDS as though all this was something of a jaunt, a holiday. Don't get that impression. I was just lucky in that the two things that put most other men out didn't worry me. Before I took to the road and started spending most of every day on my feet, I'd been doing practically the same thing every weekend on the moors, from choice, because my hobby had been rambling.

So I was used to walking. I was also used to going hungry, and for some reason I never suffered any hunger pangs. If I couldn't get food, I just stopped eating and never felt anything until my legs started to buckle and my head began to spin, but that was from weakness. So I didn't really suffer like the other chaps, the city men. They'd never walked further than the nearest pub or employment exchange and one day, without equipment, without proper shoes or clothing, off they'd gone. It must have been hell on earth for them.

Nowhere to go and no shelter. Say it quickly and it doesn't sound much. But think about it. Think about having an unbroken expanse of days in front of you, a thousand days of nothing. You come out of wherever you're staying, the doss house, the spike or the farmer's barn, wherever you've managed to get out of the weather. It's morning, and you have all day to fill until you can get into somewhere again that night. Snow, hail, rain, bitter cold, boiling heat, no matter what the weather, you have to spend all day in it. And the day after, and the day after that, with no end in sight. Your mind is hopeless, but off you go, moving from one spot to another, trying to find a roosting place for the night and a bite to eat. Day after day after day.

No wonder a lot of them gave up. I managed to occupy my mind by watching people around me. I always had the idea that one day I would become a writer and I used to make notes of this and that. I never used them, but it kept my mind off the weather when it was bad. For lots of others, it wasn't so easy. It was a daunting prospect for most chaps who'd never been on a moor in their life, to be kicked out of the spike knowing that the next sleeping place might be across hills deep in snow.

If you didn't mind losing a fair bit of dignity, there were several ways to get out of the weather. If you were in a small town or village, for instance, you headed for the library and got into the warm reading room, put a newspaper or magazine in front of you, propped your head on your hands and dozed. From a distance it looked as though you were reading, until your head fell on to the table with a bump.

Maybe it was part of the culture of those days, but many librarians, particularly the women, had no compassion. They knew you were sheltering, but they'd have you out. Sometimes as soon as you put your head round the door, they'd see you were neither a regular nor 'respectable', and respectable was largely a matter of polished shoes, a crease in your pants and a collar and tie. If you had none of these, there would be a finger pointing, first at you and then at the exit. I've been literally pushed and prodded to make me turn round and leave. I still feel nothing but contempt for librarians. It's irrational, I know, but there it is. I was conditioned to it.

You would find the same thing in the larger shops, places like Woolworths and Marks and Spencers. To this day, in bad weather you can still see them: some old boy leaning on a radiator, either hoping to get his clothes dry, or at least soak up a bit of warmth before being ordered out by the shop-walker, who's probably never missed a meal in his life.

There were exceptions, of course. I've known people be given meals by shop owners and staff, but the stuff about red rebels that was splashed around in the *Mail* and the *Express* made most people afraid of tramps. They did not see them as people who had been unfortunate enough to lose their jobs; no, they were in touch with Russia, menaces preparing to overthrow the great British Empire.

I'm remembering some of these menaces: old, and sometimes not-so-old men, their feet blistered and bleeding, picking old boots off dumps and tying them together with string to try and make them last a day or two, their trousers held up with string as well. Coughing. Dying of exposure. These were the menaces threatening the British Empire. These were the men who were going to overthrow the British way of life, and who were treated as such. I can picture them now, struggling along. Many should have been in a hospital bed but they had to cover their six or seven miles to get their slice of bread and a bed. Yes, they really had to do it: another night in the open would probably polish them off.

A great many didn't make it. A great many found they just couldn't go another step. And what did they do then, these menaces to the British Empire? They slipped out of sight like an animal and quietly died in the hedge backings.

When the daytime weather was really bad, wet or cold, or both, my way out of it was to pitch my tent somewhere out of the way. If I had a copper or two I would buy a loaf and a piece of cheese. You could buy a loaf for tuppence and half a pound of cheese for about threepence or fourpence. Then I would roll up in my blanket sleeping bag and sleep all day, which was easy, because I was usually sleep-starved. Sleeping at night in the noise and smell of a spike or a doss house took a lot of getting used to.

Sharing a room with 50 others in the doss house, nine-tenths of them ill, very often with lung trouble, made sleep almost impossible. Coughing, wheezing, snoring, moaning, talking in their sleep, waking up screaming with nightmares. I only ever catnapped all the time I was in a doss house. It was similar, but not quite as bad, in the workhouse spikes. They were kept cleaner and the dormitories were not as overcrowded.

So, rolled up on some lonely moor, hidden in a gully where the gamekeepers wouldn't spot my tent, I could sleep all day and sometimes all night. In this way I often slept the bad weather through.

Keeping clean was a big problem on the road. You're better off clean so you are not forever scratching. Some spikes would not let you in until you'd agreed to have a bath. But washing, just plain washing your hands and face was quite a problem. If you'd got a bit of soap it was not so bad, but even then you'd have to be circumspect. Out on the moors, if you started soaping yourself, the nice little brook you'd found might be being used for sheep or cattle. It has dire effects on sheep and cattle, does soapy water. The farmer would object, and who could blame him?

Some doss houses had no washing facilities, but most spikes at least had one or two tin basins that you could fill at a tap and put on a shelf to have a wash in cold water with your bit of soap. But it presented quite a few problems, did keeping clean. And so did keeping your money. There wasn't much thieving in the spikes, but, oh, those doss houses! As I have already said, I used to go in with nothing, having hidden everything outside town except fourpence to pay the doss house, or sixpence for a bed, tuppence or threepence for an evening meal or breakfast.

After paying it over, I'd have nothing left but what I stood up in. But they wouldn't let you sleep in your boots, and how were you going to stop somebody nicking those? The trick, I very soon learned, was to take the two legs at the bed head and put one leg in each boot, so that anybody who wanted one had to lift the bed, which would wake you. It has been known for two people to lift the bed from both sides, very gently, and get the boots that way. But rarely.

It was a constant battle to avoid being robbed one way or the other. One tramp legend was that you could go to bed fully dressed, with your coat buttoned up over your waistcoat, and a particularly clever thief could steal your waistcoat without waking you. A myth, of course, on a par with the old First World War soldiers who claimed the Egyptians could shave you while you were asleep.

There was a fair bit of rough stuff, too. Not so much in the spikes, where people were usually in no fit state for fighting. But in the doss houses you would find other people besides travellers. Navvies, for instance, people with temporary jobs who were using the doss house as cheap accommodation.

I'd gone to a doss house in Yorkshire and heard a racket going on. I opened the door and there was this navvy, must have been nine feet tall and five feet wide!

He'd got his boots on his fists and was lashing out with the hobnailed bottoms. Phew! Nobody could get out because he was blocking the doorway.

I slammed the door, and ran up the passageway to the bloke on the door: "This navvy's killing everybody in there!"

Barely looking up, he said, "Oh, he's all right, he'll fall over in a minute and we'll put him to bed. It's only the red biddy that's doing that."

I was outside wondering whether to risk going back in, when the row suddenly died down. Back in the dormitory, there they all were, some washing blood off their faces, others putting the navvy to bed to sleep it off.

I had one or two bits of scuffles of my own. One chap took a dislike to me. He wasn't a traveller, he was a casual labourer, working in the town and living in the doss. I'd hardly spoken to anybody in two nights except to say how do. But he kept needling me across the table. I'd got a slice of fried bread and a mug of water and I think he wanted to know was tea not good enough for me.

I told him I didn't drink tea. "Oh!" he said. "Is there something wrong with you?" And so it went on, picking and picking at me. I took no notice of him, but when I got up from the table, he jumped up and started thrusting his chest into me, and saying, "Are you yellow? Are you soft or something?" I wasn't. I'd been in boxing clubs and knew a bit about how to look after myself. It was time to tell him what he was in plain English, and he didn't like it at all. He started dancing round with his fists up. He made to hit me and came in close. I dodged him. He wasn't a boxer, anybody could have dodged him. Then I trod on his toe. I'd got my heavy boots on, my old army boots – used to buy them for half a crown. I dug my heel right into his toe. He just stood there. You never heard anybody howl so loud in your life. Blarting away like a pregnant camel he was, but it finished him off fighting. He went off to his bed mumbling about his solicitor.

I've always found, both then and since, that the best way to stop a fight is to do something desperate which they haven't seen before. If you have command of a few very painful incapacitating stunts that not many folk have seen before, it's very effective. It's the shock that stops them, as much as the pain. In various gymnasiums when I was younger, well-qualified people had shown me all sorts of rough-house stunts: the best way to stop a fight is to put the other fellow on the floor or to incapacitate him; kick him under the kneecap or something. It stops them. They don't come again.

This got me out of quite a deal of trouble in the doss houses and on the road. Town louts or farm labourers were good at the tormenting lark. They would push you, shove you and bump you with their shoulders, trying to get you to stand up to them. They knew the average tramp was either peaceable, or incapable through weakness. I would stand it for a minute or two and then pull some stunt and leave them sitting on their behind, and walk on. I used to get a certain amount of pleasure out of it. But you couldn't deal with a gang. When four or more were coming at you, you had to out-distance them fast, get within sight of houses or people.

It's just as rough nowadays with all these young muggers about, but then, as a tramp, you were a natural target. As I said earlier, it was no holiday.

CHAPTER 14

THE VISIBLE POOR

Condemned house (photograph Paul Graney).

THERE used to be two nations, the rich and the poor. The poor had a certain amount of pride. They didn't flaunt their poverty; they kept it inside their houses. They would fight for more money, better conditions, but they at least had a roof over their head, a butty on the table, and one reasonable suit. They could walk out and be what convention deemed respectable. They certainly would not roam the streets drawing attention to the fact that they were poor.

But this is exactly what the tramp and the dosser had

to do. They wore the uniform. They were the third nation of the 1920s and 1930s – the visible poor. And they were rejected by both the other nations. The rich were frightened that they would have to pay for their subsistence; the respectable poor reacted out of a different fear, that they might end up in the same plight.

There was a lot of antagonism, viciously fostered by the media, that the men on the road were workshy layabouts, and unless people had someone in the family who was in the same situation, they believed it. In those days [*the early 1920s*] the majority of people unquestioningly believed whatever was in print. You could have made a success of a square earth society if only it had been in the newspapers.

One of the most depressing and demoralising things about being on the road was the attitude of other people, knowing that practically everybody you passed in the street, everyone you dealt with, be it shopkeeper, doss house keeper, spike manager or librarian, had this fear of and contempt for the tramp. The rich were so far above us that they never entered into our sphere of things. Of the two groups I think I would rather deal with the rich. Those living in poverty could often be very callous. To the poorer people and the middle classes, you were no more than a cockroach on the wall.

Once I saw a collapsed dosser, half-hidden under the arch of a bridge. Passers-by were just striding over his legs, unwilling to acknowledge he was there. I went up to him and he was in a bad way. It looked like his heart to me. He couldn't get up, he was absolutely helpless. To give them credit, some people might have thought he was drunk, but they should have checked. A drunken man I will leave where he lies, but I find out first if he is drunk.

A couple of women, well-dressed, and well-fed, were walking past. I'd got my coat pillowed under his head, and he was blue and gasping. They could see that he wasn't drunk, and I said, "Ladies, will you ring the police and an ambulance?" And one of them said, "He's only a tramp, why should we?" I had a hell of a job keeping my mouth shut as I watched them walk away. I'd have landed in jail for a month if I'd said it. I often wonder what those two women thought about the incident. They probably went home and told their husbands they had been accosted by a dirty old tramp.

Anyway, eventually a policeman saw us and called an ambulance. The dosser was taken to hospital, but I was taken to the police station and cross-examined for an hour and a half. "Who was the bloke?"

"I don't know, I just saw him there."

"Well, who are you? Where do you come from? What are you doing? Why?"

They went on and on at me as if they thought I was a spy or something. It didn't seem to matter to them that I'd been playing the good Samaritan. I was a Means Test dosser, but they just looked at me and lumped me in with all the others, the down-and-outs, the misfits. If you were on the road you were no good. The media had fostered this view and ordinary people (including the police) had swallowed it.

So, as I've said before, they used the law that made it a crime to be without money and ran you in for wandering abroad with no visible means of subsistence. And once they'd proved you had no money, by searching you, they would probably charge you with begging. Sometimes it felt as though even breathing was a crime.

And what had brought you to this sorry state of

affairs? You'd lost your job, that's all – but so had two and a half million others. So you were part of a big problem and the Government-toadying media distracted the working population's attention from it by giving them something to feel smug about. 'These are the men who won't work' the newspapers declared. 'They're lazy good-for-nothings.' They were believed, of course, and the police were the defenders of the lie.

If you were on the road you were a 'won't-work'. Everything was weighted against you. Everything.

CHAPTER 15

FOOD FOR THOUGHT

IT IS NOT easy to survive in a civilised world without money. Out in the fields and hills you can live on nature to a limited degree. You can stay alive. But in the cities and towns, it's very difficult. So, in the 1930s, all sorts of expedients were used to get food. These included begging and even going through dustbins to salvage scraps that had been thrown out.

Some churches used to give a bowl of soup or a round of bread and cheese to children, once a day, and the Salvation Army set up soup kitchens too. But they were limited by lack of money. It was first come, first served and people would stand most of the night for the chance of a small cup of soup.

Then there was Chowbent. Chowbent is a Lancashire district near Leigh. But then it was also the nickname of Police Inspector Bent, some of whose books can be seen in the Manchester local history library. Using money from various charitable organisations, he set up the first soup kitchen in Old Trafford, in the yard of the police station in Northumberland Street.

I went once. Today, even hungry people would form a line. But people were not queue-conscious in those days, hence a huge mass of people, all struggling and pushing and only the biggest and strongest getting to the front. Between 11am and noon every day, you would find

Northumberland Street jam-packed with men, women and children, all with their bowls. Some had little four-pint buckets, like paint tins, with handles and lids, obviously hoping to get enough soup to take home to their families.

But they had to contend with this great mob, with several policemen trying to pull the children and women out to the front. I can't remember whether I got in. I know a lot of people never did. The soup ran out before they got near it. It was highly disorganised. Inspector Bent must have seen the flaws in the system and he started to open other places to ease the load.

One was in the big cellar under a branch library near Hulme Church, not far from where I lived. This one wasn't so bad. The Boys Brigade from Hulme Hall helped and they managed to set up a proper queue system – a single line down some steps and around the walls to the soup bowls. Some would take their soup home, but a lot of the younger end, of whom I was one, would just sit on the floor wherever there was a space. You would see a whole mass of people, men and lads mostly, but a few girls and women too, sitting or standing, mopping up the soup and hoping to get back in the queue for another bowl. It was a degrading procedure. But if you were hungry, you didn't bother. There used to be a saying, an empty belly has no pride, and it's true.

But the shops helped out. The smaller ones had a rapport with the working class, and some of the bigger ones were run by great philanthropists like old man Yates. He had a big cattle farm just outside Macclesfield, but is better known for his name on Yates's Wine Lodges. What is not so well known nowadays, however, is that wherever he opened a wine lodge, and every big town had at least one, a door or two away he would open a teetotal tavern, which sold only tea, coffee and food. The bakehouse of the one in Oldham Street, Manchester, had a big window backing on to Tib Street, where you could stand and watch them cutting the meat up and making pies, bread and muffins.

If you had money you could eat on the ground floor, sitting on long benches at tile-topped trestle tables. For a copper or two, you got a reasonable meal – a pie and a cup of tea. But if you could only raise a penny, you went upstairs, where there was sawdust on the floor, iron tables with chipped marble tops and planks across barrels to sit on. At a long counter you got a really deep enamel bowl, as big as a bucket; put your penny down and they would fill the bowl with soup, thick with vegetables and meat. Really good.

There was also fresh-baked bread, broken into big lumps and dumped into big baskets. You slid your bowl of soup along and got yourself as much bread as you wanted. Stuffed it down your shirt and in your pockets. I used to take a lot home. Tea, the same brand as downstairs, was a halfpenny a cup. So for a penny, one and a half pence if you wanted a drink as well, you could fill yourself up for the day. No one seemed to worry about the bread that was taken away in people's pockets. I think they all had orders to look after the poor.

But it was too much of a good thing and the business types spoiled it. Shop managers and office workers, reasonably well-to-do people, started going upstairs for a cheap meal and taking lots of free bread home in their brief-cases. Very often there would not be enough left for the out-of-works and the down-and-outs. Yates's started to cut back on the upstairs meals and eventually it stopped altogether.

Then there was the dosser's wedge, brought out first by Price's, a multiple confectioner's with a bakery at Failsworth. I never knew what the shops called them, but each one started as a pastry case, 15 to 18 inches across and about two inches deep, filled to the top with mashed-up, stale cake – a horrible looking thing. I think they were confined to North Manchester and I have only met one person who remembered them.

A few years back they reappeared as wine slices, all prettied up with an iced and decorated top and rum essence or some other flavour to mask the taste. But in the 30s they sold these big circular things, really heavy and soggy. For a penny you were given practically a quarter of it. It was a good man who could eat a whole dosser's wedge. It really took some getting down. When you'd eaten it you didn't want any more food that day. If you couldn't manage the wedge, for a halfpenny, you could get a tram-stopper, which was half the size. I think those were for the girls!

Price's Bakery also operated a system of returns. They had scores of cake shops and in the morning the vans would go out early to stock them up, bringing back all the stales, cakes that had been damaged and were unsaleable, pies that looked as though rats had been at them. They would tip it all on the floor of the bakery yard, and when they'd gone off to clean down the vans, a bloke would open the yard gates, and in would swarm a milling mob of screaming ragged-arsed, bare-foot kids, lots of them carrying paper bags to take the stuff away.

I had only two or three goes at it and that was enough. I think I got a couple of handfuls of cake, perhaps a dozen cakes and cream buns all mashed into one lump. Bread you left alone. But Price's made good pies. If you found one that had only been trodden on or dropped, you were lucky. Lots had been nibbled by rats, so you would break off the damaged part and put the other in your bag. But eventually this crazy free-for-all had to be stopped.

A good place for food was the Smithfield wholesale fruit market. When we lived close by, my mother used to buy a lot of cheap fruit and vegetables there from traders who sold to people they knew, although they were not really retail shops. Or, if you could not even afford that, you could wait until the market closed at about 10am and nip in before the cleaners arrived with their brushes and hosepipes. The traders left behind bruised apples and pears, oranges that were just going off and very often whole crates of potatoes, peas and cabbages. And the police would turn a blind eye to the scavenging.

Bread then was about threepence for a two-pound loaf and when it was two or three days old it was no longer returnable, so the shops would sell them off for a penny, half that for a small one. My mother would buy these when we were hard up. She would soak them in milk and bake them again, and they would come out, not as good as new, but soft and quite palatable.

As for meat, there was what we used to call the butcher's Saturday night. There may have been fridges in some of the big places, but I never saw one in a local butcher's, instead they had ice delivered every morning. At the bottom of Miller Street in Manchester was an ice factory. Its horse-drawn carts went out as far as Stockport, carrying blocks of ice about three feet long and 18 inches square. A butcher would have a cold room, a large insulated cupboard, to store the meat in hot weather, packing ice into it to try to keep the meat fresh.

On Saturday night, with all Sunday to get through without ice, they wanted no meat left on the premises. Shops were open officially until 8pm, but those selling perishables would stay open a lot later. I can remember going with my mother and sister to a butcher's in town. We would hang about outside till as late as 10pm, watching the prices coming down and down. The butchers, in striped aprons and straw hats, would come to the door and shout out the prices. The trick was to keep your nerve, hanging on for another copper or two off the price, but you could come unstuck. You might be waiting for a bit of stewing steak to drop another tuppence or so and somebody would jump in and get it. But if there were no buyers, the butcher would eventually almost give it away, because it was going to spoil by Monday anyway.

Some of the cinemas used to help out a bit. The Coliseum at Ardwick Green and the Triangle down Stretford Road were nothing more than little bug huts, but they had matinees and if you were out of work you could show your card and get in for a penny, *and* get a cup of tea and some biscuits. On special occasions, the Coliseum even gave out a meat pie instead of the biscuits.

Biscuits at that time were sold out of big square seven-pound tins and the shopkeeper usually ended up with perhaps four ounces of broken biscuits in the bottom of each tin. Some grocers would give these away to kids. Others would charge a halfpenny for a one-pound bagful – quite a lot of crumbs, but a fair number of nearly whole biscuits too.

But all in all, the food business was very precarious. You could find yourself eating bad eggs, for instance. In some shops, usually the multiple grocers, if they had a cracked egg they would put it in a bowl, just as it was. For the price of one normal egg you could usually get half a dozen or a dozen of these cracked eggs, if you took a basin with you.

But into the bowl, which was sometimes an enamel bucket, went all the bad eggs as well. So you tried to pick out those which were cracked but which hadn't run. Of course, someone else had usually been there before you and what was left was just a thick, runny mess of shells and broken yolks. You dipped your hands into this gooey mess and scooped your bowlful, doing the best you could with it. Omelettes could be made out of it, or spoonfuls fried in a pan. You got quite used to eating bad eggs too!

If you were not very proud and you weren't too faddy, you could get by. That was the pattern of the Shirtless Thirties – people struggled and survived – some of them. The main trouble was the feeling of hopelessness. You could see no end to it. After two, three or four years, you began to think this was how it would be for the rest of your life. When you're living at the very bottom, the only way you can look is left. But we'd had a taste of a Labour Government and couldn't see any hope in that – George Lansbury and that crew.

At the beginning, you had a certain amount of hope. But after years of either no jobs, or jobs lasting only a few weeks, and still no sign of anything better on the horizon, you sometimes felt it was no use going on. But most of us did, of course.

CHAPTER 16

A PENNY FOR 'EM

AS THE 30s ground onwards and the decline in money-making jobs continued, the penny and the half-penny came to be more important than ever, to the unemployed and the poor. A penny. It may sound very little, but believe me, it could make the difference between eating and going hungry. I've known grown men work all morning for a penny or a halfpenny, just to get a bit extra.

For a penny you could buy a stale two-pound loaf. If you could raise another few pence, you could buy eight ounces of margarine and you were set for the week. A bit of wood to keep the fire going and you'd got toast. It was poor, it was monotonous, but you ate, you stayed alive, and all on a matter of pennies.

So what kind of casual jobs were there? Well, one dodge, particularly among the older end, because it was tough work, was white-washing backyards. In narrow-entried, poorer areas of Manchester such as Hulme, Ancoats and Collyhurst, the houses had tiny backyards ending at a wall with a gate in it, on the other side of which was an entry about three and a half feet wide. Across that was another wall, another tiny yard and the back of another terraced house.

The houses, so close together and not having big windows, were consequently very dark. So to gain a bit of light by reflection, it was popular to whitewash the backyard walls and the house wall, usually up to the level of the bedroom window ledges. You can still see a few of these whitewashed yards, if you know where to look. Anyway, where there was a job, there'd be someone offering to do it for a couple of bob. Armed with a bucket of lime, a brush and a stepladder, blokes would go from house to house, and could make a fair living off it.

The trouble was that most of these chaps were on the dole and if they were found doing it, not only did they have their dole stopped, they also faced prosecution. One chap I knew had the worst possible luck: he knocked on a door which was answered by the clerk at the labour exchange where he signed on.

Busking was another money maker, though fewer tried it. In those days you were allowed to busk outside theatres and in certain streets. You could sing with a placard round your neck – Out of Work with 99 Kids – and hold out your cap in the minor shopping streets. On Ancoats Lane you could hire a barrel organ for the day, providing you paid the deposit. I well remember one old Italian chap who had his own genuine barrel organ, the little box on a stick, with a handle, and a monkey sitting on top. He was around before the war, and then just disappeared. It was a popular supposition that all these buskers had lots of loot stashed away, but I doubt it. I knew some of them and the way they lived and I don't think their death duties would amount to much.

Only the pawn-brokers got rich, because so many people used the shops with the three-ball symbol. Every Monday you'd see queues of women with big bundles, tied up in old tablecloths or bedding, waiting for 'Uncle' to open the pop shop. About 50 or 60 of them, every Monday the same ones. Their husband's best suit, sons' and daughters' shoes, frocks and suits, whatever they had that was worth money, was taken in. They lost money on it, but still they did it.

And of course, when Friday came and they had their wages, everybody wanted their clothes back to go out at the weekend. So, come Friday night or Saturday morning, they'd be at the shop again to get them out, at full price, of course. He was not in business for the love of it. You were leaving your bundle as security against a loan, and loans cost money.

It was silly. If only they'd pulled themselves straight one week, but they never did. It was a way of life, a habit. Come Monday morning, even if they had enough money to last them the week, they would look at their husband's suit hanging there, and think, there's five or six shillings there doing nowt. And off they'd go. It was a vicious system.

There were hundreds of pawn shops in Manchester. In Hulme alone, there must have been 50 or 60 and they all did a good trade. I don't think there were any poor pawnbrokers. We never went near them. Weekly payments neither; my mother used to say: "If we can't pay for it, we'll do bowt, lad." And we did.

But one group of people did make the odd penny or two out of the pawn shops – the young kids. They really were the most inventive money-makers. They would take the pawn shop bundles in, for people who were ashamed to be seen there, or who did not want to go, for whatever reason. They got quite well organised in the end – they had boxes with wheels and handles that would take perhaps half a dozen bundles at once. Uncle would pay them a commission. I even knew a grown man doing it.

It was surprising what lads aged between 10 and 14 got up to, sometimes quite illegally. One dodge, quite dangerous, was searching railway carriages. When a train came in, if it had finished its trip, it would be shunted into the sidings, which were easily accessible at Central Station and London Road. The kids would hide, then climb into the carriages and search them before the cleaners arrived. There were all sorts of things to be found: lost wallets, cases, dropped money, even packets of uneaten sandwiches. But eventually one lad was knocked down and badly injured and a week or two later another was killed. So they put watchmen on duty to keep the kids away.

Another illegal stunt, usually to get cinema money, was to climb into the back yard of a pub, nick a few empty bottles, then go to the off-licence counter at the front, bold as brass, and claim the halfpenny deposit on each one. At some picture houses you could get admission for a couple of jam jars, so kids would go looking for them. There were none to be found in dustbins – with a penny on the big 'uns and a halfpenny on the little 'uns, nobody threw them away. You had to ask, or 'find' them illegally.

There were also hundreds of small gambling schools. Every street corner had a pitch and toss game. Around Hulme, in the Silver Street area, the police walked together in twos, and in threes on Saturday nights. It was rough. But sharp young lads who had scraped together a few pence would be in there with the older lads and men, playing pitch and toss for halfpennies.

The system was that if you got in a game and lost your money, you could go on crow. In Collyhurst they called it on dog. In other words, you were a lookout. From the next corner, you watched for the police and whistled when you saw them. And for every game played, a halfpenny was put aside for the crow man. So you stayed on crow until you'd got yourself another stake, threepence or whatever, and you were back in the game.

Later at night the game would be cards, in someone's house. I've seen blokes start with threepence or fourpence and play from 7pm till 1am, all for coppers – just another attempt to make a penny or two.

CHAPTER 17

KIDS' STUFF

Picnic (photograph Paul Graney).

MONEY did not come easily for most kids. They earned their money either through some clever dodge, or officially, by working. There was a lot of exploitation, a prime example being the lads who did paper rounds for newsagents. There were not many, mainly because of the conditions. They would work all week, out at 6am in all weathers, winter and summer, on terrific rounds, three or four miles long. Then they'd be out again with the evening papers – Manchester had two, the *Evening*

Chronicle and the *Evening News* – and for all this they would earn about a shilling a week. It was desperate.

Or you could take your chance as a fly newspaper seller, running through the streets with a bundle tucked under your arm. Anyone could go to the Chron office in Withy Grove or the News office in Cross Street and get a bundle. If they were daily regulars they would be trusted with them. Otherwise they had to pay for what they took. I can still remember them dashing through the terraces, bawling out: "Chron and News! Chron and News!" People who'd missed getting one at their usual place would bob their head out of the door and buy one.

Saturday was the big night. As soon as the last editions of the evening papers were gone, the weekend *Umpire* put out its Manchester edition. It later became the *Empire News*, now long since gone. You could buy it soon after 5pm outside the cinemas and stations, and from lads and blokes running past shouting, "Umpire!" You could almost tell the time by them.

How much they earned I don't know, but they must have thought it worthwhile because there was a lot of competition for the papers and you were carefully vetted by the bloke who dished them out. It was all on trust. He just gave you the number of papers you asked for and you went back Monday morning and paid him. One or two wide boys would manage to get a handful, pocket the money and never appear again, but that finished them. They could never go again.

I never sold papers, but I know there were a lot of rules to be observed if you didn't want your clock knocking round. Everyone had his own beat and I've seen fights when someone with just a few papers left would try to sell them on someone else's beat. The bloke who owned the beat would do a bit of thumping, or get his pals to do it for him.

Manchester was not short of small-time gangsters, as I've already indicated. At one period they waged war with the chaps who sold papers from regular pitches in the city. The bully boys would wait till the last paper was sold, then go along and grab the money off them. Of course, the sellers did not all take it lying down and in the end, what with all the pitched battles, the newspapers cleaned things up. The accredited sellers were licensed to have their stands and were given badges of police protection.

If they did not mind working, there were lots of other ways for kids to make money. Running errands for a shop, for instance. Delivered goods were a sort of status symbol for both the customer and the shop. Only the rich were supposed to want their goods delivered. The main shops generally employed a lad who rode a big iron bike with a basket on the front, but small corner shopkeepers who didn't have a delivery boy would simply go to the door and shout to the nearest group: "Anybody want a penny?" You'd be given a big basket and an address and off you'd go. Kill yourself doing it, but you'd earned a penny, or maybe not ... I had two or three pals who delivered orders for a corner shop in the evenings and were paid in groceries to take home. They would get perhaps a loaf, a pound of margarine, or some boiled ham, according to what the job was worth.

Coal delivering was another stunt. The normal horse-drawn cart carried big sacks of coal and if you were in steady work you could get a bag of coal a week for about a shilling and ninepence. But if you couldn't afford a full bag, there was a small coal yard in every second street. The bloke who ran it would have a heap of loose coal, perhaps five or six hundredweight, plus a set of scales and three or four little trucks. They weren't barrows. I've never since seen anything like them. They must have been designed specially. A stout wooden box, slightly wider at the top was set on two iron wheels, and an iron bar with a crosspiece – a bit like a scout's trek cart.

If you were poor, you would go to the yard, buy a quarter [*twenty-eight pounds*] of coal, have it tipped into the cart, and away you'd go. This again was all on trust. There was never any charge for the carts, but they were always brought back. For three or four pence you could buy about ten pounds of coal. I forget the exact prices, but it was very cheap.

Many people either wouldn't or couldn't pull their own coal home, so there was always the chance of picking up a halfpenny. You could knock on doors where you were known: "Do you want any coal fetching, missus?" At the yards, you would see kids queuing for a cart. Heavy work, but worth it for the odd copper.

Even harder was the work to be had at the stations. Lads aged ten and upwards, a few even younger, would haunt the approaches to Central, London Road or Exchange Stations, or the main entrance to Victoria. A train would unload and there'd be passengers hurrying for buses to get across town, and the kids would swarm around them: "Carry your bag, Sir?" "Carry your bag, Miss?" It was pitiable – some kids were so small and the cases so heavy that you'd see them practically dragging them along, struggling and panting.

And you daren't ask for money. I've done it myself many a time, struggling along with cases that seemed to be packed with bricks. You'd be dragging behind, and the bloke would be away in front, shouting, "Come on, lad,

I've got a bus to catch." Your arms would be dropping off and you'd get to the bus station and he'd say, "Well thank you, that's been a big help." And there you were. But as often as not you would get a few coppers, a penny or tuppence, for carrying the bags. You worked for it. You were in competition with all these other kids, and there were literally scores of them.

The big snag was that the small-time gangsters I've already mentioned soon cottoned on to this as another way to make easy money. If you were bag-carrying, you'd make a day of it. You'd be at the station from the first train in, perhaps 8am or so, and you'd be hanging about until the last, which could be 9pm or later.

The gangsters, of course, depended on spies, other little raggedy-arsed kids who skulked about, watching who was doing well. At the end of the day, they'd point them out and the bully boys would catch hold of them, bang them on the earhole and make them hand over. The kids would be left without a light, for all the work they had done. Sometimes they would hide, sloping off down back alleyways. But once you'd done that, you couldn't go back to the same stunt. They'd be watching for you.

There was another railway racket, very good when it worked, but very chancy. It was based on the anomalies in train fares. I might be wrong in the exact figures, but a day return from London to Manchester was about twelve shillings and sixpence and amazingly enough, that was at least two shillings cheaper than the single fare. So of course, people did not buy a single ticket, but a day return and at London Road they were left with the return half. So all the kids would cluster on the approach: "Got a return half, mister?" And eventually, if you were lucky, you'd be given one – a ticket to London. And with one of these in your hand you were in. You could easily sell it for five shillings because people going to London would actually be looking for you: "Anybody got a return half?" They might be paying you a dollar [*five shillings*], but they'd be saving themselves quite a lot of money.

The kids could make themselves as much as ten shillings or a pound, especially on Saturdays. This went on for a long time, until the railways latched on to it and adjusted the fares.

But of course, the gangsters' little spies had their eyes on this dodge, too, marking you out. If they saw you do a deal, that was it. The only way was to disappear, and fast. I remember once I'd sold a return for a dollar. Untold riches! A fellow could buy a gold-plated Rolls-Royce with five shillings! But I could see these two grubby little kids watching, and when one suddenly disappeared, I knew he'd gone for his gang.

I fled. I bought a penny platform ticket. London Road had a half-mile platform, ending in a bridge where you could cross to Mayfield Station. I raced all the way, over the bridge, into Mayfield, out into Ashton Old Road, and all the way to Droylsden, started cutting across the fields at Failsworth towards Salford then back home from Salford into Hulme. But it finished me. I didn't dare go back to the station. They would have knocked me senseless.

My first really bad experience with the gangs came when I was just turned 16 and working – I think I was earning about ten shillings a week. A lad I knew said he made himself a few extra shillings a week by working every night and Sunday mornings, bundling firewood in a tumbledown wooden shanty on a croft in Salford. The boss used an old circular saw to cut bits of timber into five-inch sticks. The kids were employed to bundle it, counting so many sticks and twisting a length of soft wire round them.

I went to watch. Talk about slave labour! My mate and the other lads were cutting their fingers to pieces. And they didn't get paid so much an hour, or even so much a dozen bundles. They got a penny per 100 bundles. If they were lucky they'd complete 200 in two hours. Oh no, I thought, not for me.

Even so, not long afterwards, six of us decided to try the firewood lark ourselves, as there was always lots of wood knocking about. In Trafford Park you could get all the old packing cases you could carry. They burned them, but if you went along to the yard they would let you have them. There were always streams of blokes coming out of Trafford Park early in the morning, loaded with planks and boards and packing cases, like so many smugglers. The same applied to a lot of the engineering firms in town, and many old warehouses also had burnable junk.

Once we had our stock of timber and knew where to go for more, we set to with a couple of old saws and two or three borrowed axes. Then we loaded our bundles into a couple of trucks made of Tate and Lyle sugar boxes on old pram wheels and set off round the streets selling four bundles for a penny, half the shop price.

We were soon doing quite nicely, making three or four shillings each per week. It was a lot of work. We would start early in the morning and still be going round the streets at 9.30pm and 10pm. In between, we would be sawing and chopping and bundling. A hell of a lot of work, but we didn't mind as long as we could see something for it.

But whenever a profitable scheme showed up, so did the gangsters. We bigger lads worked in an old yard that we'd acquired for the production of the bundles, and in the afternoons and after tea, the young lads of about ten or eleven would be off selling around the streets. But pretty soon it became a regular thing for them to come back crying, having been beaten up by bully boys, who'd taken their trucks, their wood and any money they'd made.

It all ended early one night when a group of hefty 17 and 18-year-olds invaded our yard. How murder wasn't done I'll never know. There were four or five or us with axes in our hands when these bully boys charged in, smashed everything up, searched us, grabbed all the money, and gave us all a beating. I lashed out at more than one with my axe but I still got a good thumping.

That was the end of the firewood lark. The gangsters took it over. Where we had been giving the kids a fair share of the money, they thumped them if they didn't go out, and gave them a penny or two instead of a shilling. They tried to make us do the work as well, but we weren't having that. We disappeared.

It was a blight on us all, this petty gangsterism, but there was one area where the bully boys couldn't make any headway – the markets, which at that time were pretty free and open. Ninety per cent of the foodstuffs arriving at Smithfield in Manchester came from local farms on lorries, with the occasional horse-drawn wagon. They couldn't get right inside to the stalls, so they parked on the outside. It was very badly congested.

A driver, having parked, would be faced with getting all his produce to the stall of whoever was buying it. But there were scores of hefty, strong blokes knocking about, blokes who could carry a hundredweight of potatoes at a fast run. Some worked for particular stalls, others were sort of freelancers. The lorry driver would pick one of them and pay him to carry his spuds or cabbages or whatever to the stall. Big hefty lads, as I say, and the gangsters had learned not to tangle with them. Even so, there was a lot of trouble; what you might call internal strife.

Three in the morning was the average starting time, and you'd finished by 10am. So one of the strong-arm porters would be waiting for his usual lorry and when it arrived a lad would be sitting next to the farmer. He'd flagged him down on his way in and offered to do the job cheaper. Naturally, there were fights, lots of them, and in the end the market organisers stepped in and only licensed porters were allowed. It stopped a lot of the trouble. Good thing too, it was chaos.

About this time, I got involved with a sort of early commune. About six of us who knew and trusted each other had got together. Inside a yard on Moss Lane, Hulme, we had found an old building , a former works of some sort, in fairly good condition, with water and even one or two fireplaces. A thick flour or grain sack, opened up, makes a good warm blanket after a lot of soaking and washing. We collected enough sacks and pieces of sacks to make up some beds. We occupied this building and as we trusted one another, we more or less lived together. We didn't steal each other's food and if we had a bit more than we needed, we would share it.

One day, the bully boys broke in and stole all the sacking. We found the windows shattered, the door broken in, even floorboards pulled up, out of sheer vandalism. We didn't give up. We got more sacks and started again. We demolished the stairs and moved on to the first floor, with a loft ladder we could haul up behind us. That stopped the vandals. It was fairly comfortable and reasonably warm, even in bad weather, once you were rolled up in your sacking. I lived there for several months.

I was living on the money that I earned at the George and Dragon pub, next to Hulme Church. On Saturday and Sunday nights the upstairs room was open for a real beer-swilling weekend. On Monday morning, I would move in and clear the place up: mop the floor, clean the glasses, the lot. It would take all day from about 9am, but I earned fourpence and I could live all week on that, along with the free food that we managed to obtain from the Smithfield leftovers.

I never really had the will or the ability to chase odd jobs, but for a while I did a thing that suited my abilities; running in the pigeons, it was called. At that time, lots of people kept a few pigeons in the back yard, in home-made lofts patched up out of orange boxes. And every street corner had its own pigeon-racing club, perhaps 20 or 30 men who would put their entrance fees together, get a basket, put the pigeons in it and send them off to be released at some distant railway station.

Deciding the winner was not done by fancy clocks. When the pigeon returned to its home loft, it was up to its owner to entice it in and take the identity ring off its leg. They used to spend hours trying to train the birds to come straight in, sending them out hungry as often as not, then rattling corn to tempt them in.

Once they had the ring, they would hand it to a runner if they couldn't run themselves. Most couldn't – but I could. I had a reputation as a runner. I was in an athletic club. They'd give me the ring and off I'd race to the flying club's headquarters, usually the back kitchen of a house in the area. First ring in was the winner, whether the bird was first home or not. You could get tuppence, sometimes threepence a run. If you were on a winner it could be sixpence or more.

In the end, I was doing two runs every Sunday, one in Hulme, the other at the other side of City Road, Bedford Street, and they usually came in an hour later, so I could run for a bloke there as well. The only trouble was, I wanted the money to go camping. I needed eightpence for a weekend, fourpence tram fare to Hyde, where I set off into the hills, then fourpence home. So I eventually gave up the pigeon-running. It left me with too little time for camping.

MARCHING AND FIGHTING

CHAPTER 18

WET BLANKETS

THERE were several abortive hunger marches round about 1930, the year the *Daily Worker* appeared, and I think the *Daily Worker* did a lot of organising and collecting for the main hunger march in 1936 – the Jarrow March as it was always known afterwards. Before that, several towns organised their own marches, a few hundred-strong, but I don't think many reached London, and they were too small to make much impact anyway. So I don't know for sure when the first hunger march was held. But I do know what made the big one possible.

By 1929, I was home from my wanderings and had found a job. But it didn't last long – eight or nine months and the firm folded up. In those days you weren't given notice and there was no redundancy pay. You went for your wages to the pay office and a decent pay clerk would put your cards in your hand and tell you not to come back on Monday. But your average clerk would just stick your cards in your hand with your wages. Quite a few old men like myself still refer to being sacked as getting your lick 'ems and stick 'ems – a euphemism for getting your cards, complete with stamps.

By this time, the labour exchanges had begun to multiply. In the early days, no matter where you lived, there was only the Aytoun Street exchange off Piccadilly and people had to walk miles to sign on and draw the dole. Mine was one of the new ones, in a church hall in Alexandra Road, Moss Side.

Meanwhile, in response to the continuing jobless crisis, a fairly strong organisation, the National Unemployed Workers Movement, had also grown up, run quite legally, non-profit-making, and non-contributory, by a central committee in Manchester. And this central body, responding to the Government's example, now began to delegate smaller committees to the new exchanges, improving its organising skills as it went along.

I had sort of drifted into being a central committee member of the movement. We gave all the services we could, including advice and representation at Means Test tribunals. Or, if the breadwinner of a family lost the dole for some minor infraction, we would go with him, and try to get some money out of the National Assistance Board. These were the days when the basic grant might be eight shillings, plus two shillings and sixpence for a wife and a shilling for each child. And that was considered quite generous.

As our numbers and confidence grew, we started organising demonstrations. Mainly we were protesting against the Means Test, or Transitional Benefits as it was called, which was applied after 26 weeks on the dole. On one occasion we decided to march from Stevenson Square, off Oldham Street, Manchester. There was a people's forum there, where soap box orators provided good entertainment on Sunday afternoons.

We had our own speakers in the square. When we had something planned we would announce it there. We also had teams outside all the labour exchanges, shouting details of the demonstration or whatever. We had no money for leaflets. We would just tell as many people as possible in the week beforehand.

For the particular demonstration I'm thinking of, we wanted to go from Stevenson Square to Platt Fields and hold a mass meeting there. We'd applied to the Watch Committee and the Chief Constable for permission, describing the route, the probable number of people, the fact that we had a band and confirming that we knew the procession rules, which were that we must march neither in step, nor in fours. To have done so would have constituted unlawful assembly, marching as only the Army was allowed to do.

So we would be marching in scattered ranks and out of step, to comply with the law; and we would obey the orders of the mounted police marshals who would be making sure that we didn't disrupt the traffic. Traffic! A few railway cart-horses, a couple of milk churn carts, a few trams here and there, the odd motor car. Those were the days when you could walk in the road down Oxford Street from St Peter's Square to All Saints and never be in danger. But we would apparently disrupt the traffic if we went that way. So they gave us a new route: out of the square, down Aytoun Street, Portland Street and Whitworth Street into Princess Street. This would keep us out of the way of the main traffic, they said. It would also keep us out of the way of a lot of people, and our idea was to put our case in front of as many people as we could. But we had to do as they said.

We set off at 10.30am, the band leading, followed by the committee, including me, right in front of all the trouble as usual. We got into Aytoun Street, with the two mounted policemen leading and quite a number of police stooging up and down both sides to see that we didn't spread out too far. Near its end, Aytoun Street was flanked by a big fire station and as the band approached this, a line of firemen ran out with hoses, which they opened up on us.

Naturally, everybody tried to rush back, but whoever had plotted this had anticipated our every move. Behind us, out of the side streets behind Minshull Street Court, rushed another squad of mounted police, plus police on foot with batons. Our front end was trying to retreat from the fire hoses, and the people at the back were trying to break through to the front, away from the police baton-charge. There were over 1,000 of us. It was chaos.

Next to Aytoun Street labour exchange was a Royal Infirmary annexe. Nurses who had been watching through windows there threw them open and called to us. Those of us who were fit enough climbed over spiked railings, across the window ledges, shot through the hospital and out into the street behind London Road, and made our escape.

But from what I saw prior to this, the police were just charging about indiscriminately. There were warehouses opposite, one of them with a dozen wide steps leading up to its glass front door. Many of the office workers had heard the band and come to the top of the steps to watch us pass. One mounted policeman simply rode up those steps and started lashing out with his truncheon, not your ordinary 15-inch truncheon either, but the long one, more than three feet of hard wood. You could smash a door in with one of those. A vicious weapon.

He was up there on his horse, indiscriminately trampling people, slashing at them. Somebody died that day, probably on those steps, because I saw four or five fall and stay down. I'm sure this was the incident that Walter Greenwood wrote about in *Love on the Dole*. It still makes me fume to think that we had been given permission and were being escorted, but as soon as they had us sealed off in a quiet corner, they just laid into us.

There were the usual consequences: many of us ended up in court for disorderly conduct, or attacking the police. Quite a few went to prison for terms between 14 days and three months. Some were only fined, but they finished up in jail anyway, since they had no money to pay.

That was one of our abortive demonstrations, but by now the idea of marching to London and demonstrating outside Number 10 or the House of Commons was catching on. Various groups were trying it, but they didn't get very far, perhaps 100 miles or so, before they had to come back.

Then came the Jarrow March, the one that made the history books, organised from Tyneside on a nation-wide basis. They had asked Glasgow and various parts of industrial Scotland to start out with them from Jarrow. They were the shipyard men, whose works had been closed for months, some of them for years.

They also asked the Lancashire left-wing organisations to help and called for assistance from the unemployed organisations, which funnily enough were not all left-wing. There were a lot of left-wing people among them but the average person wasn't concerned about politics. He just wanted a bit more money to feed his kids.

So, all through the country the rallying cry went up: "March with us to London! Get your petitions organised!" I can't remember all the demands – Abolish the Means Test, Increase the Dole, that sort of thing. But it was reckoned there were 1,500,000 signatures, carried on the march in three suitcases.

Organising a march like this was not easy. We had more enthusiasm than ability. I think the Manchester contingent must have numbered about 500 or 600. It was pathetic to see them. A croft at the back of Ancoats Lane, in a small children's playground, was where we vetted the volunteers. They came in worn-out old shoes, thin clothes, old macs. We'd say to them, "Can you get hold of a blanket? Can you bring any food? Have you any money?" In most cases the answer was "No".

But you *had* to have a little money. We couldn't rely on handouts all the way, because as we got closer to London there would be thousands marching with us. We intended to meet the Jarrow lot in St Albans and the Welsh miners would head straight for London and meet us in Hyde Park. Several thousand people want a lot of feeding and most of the organisations and individuals who supported us were either poor themselves or on the dole. Collections and money-raising events did a lot of good, but it wasn't enough for such a vast number.

And some regions did not vet their volunteers as thoroughly as we did. I had insisted on this because I had the years on the road under my belt and knew what it could do. Our volunteers would have to pound along at the rate of ten miles or so a day and while many can do that, you need to be pretty fit to keep it up six or seven days a week for a couple of weeks, which was what we'd allowed ourselves.

After the first day, most people who were not accustomed to walking were stiff, and full of blisters, but they had to get up the following day and do it all over again, and all the days after that. Even so, at our vetting meetings, on that cinder-covered croft, we often failed to get it through to them. We would ask, "What is the furthest you have ever walked?" Oh dear! Most had never walked farther than the nearest pub or the dole office. They'd come in plimsolls, they said, thinking they couldn't afford decent boots. But for a couple of shillings at Lords Army and Navy Stores in Liverpool Street, you could buy patched up ex-army boots, worn but still serviceable. They needed breaking in for a week or two, otherwise you were worse off than ever, but at least they would stand up to a pounding such as this march would give them.

And food! "Oh, we'll bring some grub," they'd say. Before we started off we checked the food situation. Some had brought just what they could stuff into their pockets: a few butties, bread and jam, bread and cheese, plus a few black-and-whites – a working man's way to carry the makings of a brew: tea, sugar and condensed milk mixed together and wrapped in a twist of newspaper. They'd brought half a dozen or so for the fortnight.

Some didn't even bring a blanket to roll up in. Mind you, a blanket is not much protection if you're not under cover. Even if it doesn't rain you only need one heavy dew and it's soaked. Then if you don't walk with it spread on your back to dry it during the day you're in trouble the next night. And there definitely wasn't cover for all these people. We had offers of shelter in various village halls and church halls and underneath arches, so yes, we had planned it as best we could, but when you've got several hundred people with varying amounts of ability and disability, you can't accurately plan how far you're going to go in a day.

I think we had about £14 or £15 for emergencies, such as blokes conking out with feet so raw and limbs so stiff they couldn't go on. It happened to many and two that I remember had to quit with heart trouble. We used the money to send a telegram and then we would get them on to a train home.

We were fortunate in having enough qualified people to look after everybody's welfare: two or three male nurses, hospital-trained in first aid, plus people like me who knew about survival, how to find shelter for the more desperate cases.

CHAPTER 19

SORE FEET

SO off we went, and soon the pattern was established. By 9am each day, we'd have everyone on their feet, rousted out from wherever they were sleeping, in the hedges or from the various halls and barns that were put at our disposal. Then people would come along with packets of sandwiches for them. They often had no more money than we had, but they were prepared to sacrifice their own food for us and we dished it out as best we could, to the more deserving cases. There was never enough and this raised a lot of bad feeling: "Why has he got some and I haven't?" But after about five or six days most of the people who had not realised what they were getting into had gone, along with the grumblers and grousers.

By the time the Liverpool lads had joined up with us and the Wolverhampton and Birmingham groups, the police were watching all the time, walking with us to make sure we were not making trouble. By then, the line must have been a couple of miles long and nobody wanted to give up. Many of the marchers were trying to conceal their sore feet, blisters and swollen joints because they didn't want to be sent home. We couldn't force them, but we had to maintain a fairly steady pace. They struggled along, their feet bleeding: "No, I'm all right, don't worry about me." But they were dropping behind and splitting up the whole troop. This meant having to leave people behind to look after them.

One thing we did not anticipate was the way the

police interfered with our nightly stops in village halls and schools. We would find a line of police blocking our access into a village or town. "You can't come through the town, you'll disrupt the traffic. You'll keep the people off the street, and the shopkeepers are complaining." They concocted all sorts of stories. They also gave us bits of paper with diagrams scrawled on them, saying, "You can skirt the town if you go that way." But of course that way would take us away from the places we had planned to stop and sleep, and by this time we were several thousand strong. The first time it happened, we had got into a park. The shelters were overflowing and all the rest were under trees. At midnight, in teeming rain, along came the police, turned us all out and put a guard on the park so we couldn't return.

It happened all the way. You couldn't blame all the police. Sometimes they'd be quite sympathetic: "Sorry, lads, but this is the order. I've got to do it. It's my job." Others just sneered at us: "If you won't work, this is what you can expect." Of course, it was all media-fostered. We were the forerunners of the red hordes that were coming to overthrow the country, subsidised by Communist Russia to upset the British way of life!

In one place, on a really wet night, we had been given the use of two dance halls and one or two other halls, and several pubs had thrown their top rooms open to our desperate cases. All in all, we had managed to get about 600 under cover. The police waited until two in the morning and then turned everybody out. It was illegal, they said. The premises weren't covered for fire insurance was another excuse. It came from the top, that was obvious. It was very disheartening to find people against you like that.

But we kept on. Eventually we met the Jarrow crowd. They'd met a fair bit of trouble too, and some of the wild Scots and Tynesiders had ended up having a duffy with the policemen. They said they weren't having any nonsense with them. But of course you can't win by cracking a policeman and quite a few had landed in the nick.

In the Scousers' team there was a little thin chap of about 60, the noisiest and most vociferous of them all, but he'd absolutely conked out. Two of his mates had found a short plank, tied two ropes to it, sat him on this between them, and were carrying him. We tried to persuade him to go home but he wasn't having any of it. His feet were raw. I've never seen anything so ghastly. It was just as though somebody had skinned them. They must have been absolute agony, but he refused to give up.

Eventually his mates found an old pram on a dump, lined it with blankets, made a soft spot for him, gave him a Means Test placard and sat him there, and he was happy. He was a comical looking little man, a cheerful bloke. People were running out of pubs with pints for him. I lost sight of him in Hyde Park. I don't know what happened to him after that.

We got into Hyde Park the night before the demonstration. At first they weren't going to let us stay, then they decided that it wouldn't be safe to have thousands of people prowling the streets all night, so they relented. They ringed the park with police like a concentration camp.

In the morning I went to an exit with a sack to buy some loaves. Someone else was going for margarine and cheese and jam to make our little circle some butties for breakfast, but they wouldn't let us out at first. I demanded to see an inspector, asking, "Who's given you these orders? We've not broken any laws. Where you're standing is a public thoroughfare and any member of the public has a right to walk on it." All the usual teenage know-it-all stuff. But it worked. They let us out. We got the grub and came back.

Then the speeches started. I can't remember who all the speakers were. I think there was a journalist called Brailsford and I'm sure George Lansbury was there. But of course we didn't know any of these people by sight. And a lot of the speeches were inaudible. There were so many people, and public address systems were in their infancy. You could only shout to a couple of hundred or so through a megaphone and there were over 100,000 there, many of them out of sight, never mind out of hearing. The park was packed.

It all ended in chaos. There had already been one or two pretty savage baton charges and eventually the police cleared the park with one ferocious charge. The *Daily Herald* reported that more than 100 were severely injured and 50-odd arrested.

The petitions? Well, we found out later that the three suitcases had been put into a left-luggage office, but when they went to collect them they had unaccountably disappeared. Our chaps had the receipts for them, but they had gone. Nobody could figure out why or how. The left-luggage office just blandly said, "They're not here." And that was the end of it.

The *Daily Herald* said the loss had saved a lot of people a great deal of embarrassment. It had saved the right-wing press, for instance, from trying to prove that two-thirds of the signatures were forgeries. And it had saved the Government the embarrassment of having to deal with our case in the House of Commons. Actually we did do a bit of good. There were various alterations in dole conditions, unemployment benefits were increased by a few coppers and the Means Test itself was relaxed a little.

But the immediate result of the great march was to leave hundreds of tired people roaming about London, trying to get back home. Many stayed in the capital and went on the bum. But a lot set off to walk or hitch back. One firm of carriers offered lifts in empty vans and lorries going north and a lot of railwaymen turned a blind eye to people climbing into north-bound goods wagons.

But it still left hundreds on the road trying to get home. I was one of them. I had my tent and I teamed up with a bloke called Tommy. We'd been out for about three days, heading for Manchester, and one morning after breakfast he just packed up his gear up and said, "I'm off." Where he went, and why, I'll never know.

Anyway, that's the way the Great Hunger March finished. A bit of conniving by some of the big boys, a lot of police pressure, a lot of people left adrift, and it was all over.

CHAPTER 20

BLACKSHIRTS AND BLUDGEONS

IN 1922 there had been a march of a different kind. It was made by Mussolini, and his destination was Rome. His Fascist Party's declared aim was to assist in the preservation of law and order. And when he and his cohorts had achieved their objective, with their jackboots, rubber truncheons and castor oil bottles, they took power, with Mussolini as dictator of Italy.

This chain of events appealed to certain people in England. The thug-minded people here saw promise in such a scheme and little offshoots of various political parties began to use similar tactics, but there was nothing organised about it at first, just little gangs of people smashing up meetings of people with whom they disagreed.

Then, in 1930, MP John Beckett, in order to gain some notoriety, grabbed the mace in the House of Commons and marched out with it. It was retrieved straight away but the upshot was that another MP, multi-millionaire Oswald Mosley, teamed up with Beckett, and a few months later a new party had appeared: The British Union of Fascists, very much modelled on Mussolini's gang. They wore practically the same uniform: jackboots, black trousers and black shirts. I don't think they actually used insignia, but they carried wooden truncheons, hidden in a special trouser pocket, giving easy access. I know they were wooden, not rubber, because I was hit by one, more than once.

Mosley's gang used Mussolini's tactics of bullying and smashing up meetings. They had a lot of left-wing support in the early days: John Strachey and Harold Nicholson are two that come to mind. But as soon as their true aims and methods began to show, the Socialist backing dropped off.

They had plenty of money to spend. It must have been the industrialists who financed them, particularly when you look at their favourite target – the trades unions. I can remember vividly their American gangster methods of strike-breaking. With the collaboration of the industrialists, they would get a list of the addresses of all those on strike at a works. Then, if you worked at the firm, there would be a knock at your door one evening and standing there would be two burly, black-uniformed thugs. They would talk to you quietly and politely, pointing out how necessary it was, and how good it would be for everybody, if you went back to work. There would be no spoken threats, but only too aware of the Fascists' reputation, most people succumbed and went back to work. I've talked to a fair number of people who were visited by the blackshirts and they said the emphasis was always on the good of the country.

Then in the early 30s they followed Hitler's example and started on the Jews. Once again there was no obvious threat of personal violence and although some synagogues were desecrated or set ablaze, the Fascists denied all responsibility. I think those responsible were some of their wilder or weak-minded members, of which they had many.

Mosley never spoke of doing material damage, but he did hold provocative meetings in Jewish quarters, such as London's Whitechapel and Cheetham Hill in Manchester.

It wasn't long before various trades union and Socialist groups, the Young Communists League, the Communist party, and the Jewish community themselves, were banding together to fight back. To a certain extent this was successful, but we soon found that the Fascists had Government backing.

Mosley's men were allowed to wear uniform, for instance, which was against all regulations. Scouts and Boys' Brigades were among the very few organisations allowed to wear uniform, but the Fascists were not only allowed to do this, but to march in step, and in formation. In effect, they were a private army. Just to equip them all with uniforms and transport must have cost a fortune. It was never really established where their funds came from, but it was generally supposed that industrialists helped them, with Government approval.

I attended a good few of their meetings and the police were with them. The Fascists certainly had no need of protection early on, but there, alongside the strong-arm thugs, were British bobbies. I have seen blackshirts laying into onlookers with their wooden truncheons while the police waded into the same crowd with theirs. If you so much as lifted your fist to a Fascist, you were immediately thrown into a Black Maria and charged with disturbing the peace, causing an affray, any one of the numerous charges which could be used against you; and a judge would deal out the severest penalty allowed, with harsh words about trying to overthrow the country.

As time went on and the Fascists gained more power, it was realised that an ordinary, more or less peaceable organisation could do nothing against their organised thuggery. So many small places began to organise anti-Fascist brigades. The one I was involved in was at a long-established Socialist club, Hyndman Hall, in Liverpool Street, Salford. On its top floor was a gymnasium with a full-size ring, used by many of Salford's professional boxers. Our little anti-Fascist brigade had only about twelve members at the start, all lads who were learning amateur wrestling and boxing, with instruction from the professionals. As for me, well, one way or another I had picked up some knowledge of quarter staff combat, so I was passing on that, plus my bit of experience in general rough-housing.

One small group of a dozen could not do much good, but eventually all the little anti-Fascist groups began to work together. You couldn't get into the blackshirts' private meetings, but they held many open-air meetings, and we decided that one, on a big croft at Queens Park [*Harpurhey*], would be a good place to try out our tactics. There had been lots of publicity for the rally, on posters and via newspaper adverts, and on the day itself they marched to the park through the city, swaggering in their uniforms and singing the Fascist hymn.

I was a sort of anti-Fascist liaison officer, along with several others and we'd been round to all the people who were organising physical politics. We had found about 200 or 300 blokes willing to battle it out, but one of our troubles was lack of arms. It's not easy to acquire truncheons and billy clubs. They're made of special hard wood and are properly balanced. However, we devised a fair substitute by cutting old broomsticks into 14-inch lengths and weighting the ends by wrapping them in heavy copper wire.

It had not been easy teaching men to fight who had never been fighters, especially when the Blackshirts did not fight according to any rules but by brute force and terror. So I tried to teach our lads how to use a bludgeon, more or less police fashion, a jab to the stomach or throat, an upward blow where it hurt. Plus other tips, such as: never put your hand behind your body, always keep it in front of you; use wrist flicks rather than swinging arm blows; and never hit muscle, which will absorb a blow; aim for the wrist, the elbow, the shoulder, always where bone is exposed. I taught them simple things like this, and always to make the first move, never to be on the defensive unless they were beaten into it; get a good first crack in, so the other fellow didn't want to go on.

Anyway, we went up to Queens Park intending to hold a counter-meeting across from the Fascists and found they had a big van with two or three huge speakers on top of it. Mosley and Lord Haw-Haw were there and with their powerful amplification, none of our speakers would have been audible. So we decided to sneak round and stop the amplifiers, cut the wires, pull the leads off the batteries, anything.

Now these Fascist meetings were conducted in military style. They set up the platform for the speakers close to the van, and around these would be a double circle of blackshirts, all facing outwards, watching the crowd. Then there would be a ring of policemen, also facing outwards. And mingling with the crowd and all around the outskirts of the crowd were more police.

As soon as the blackshirts saw somebody heckling, one of them would squeeze through the crowd, bang him on the head and bundle him out for the police to pick up. If you were going to heckle you had to be well hidden behind somebody so they couldn't see you, otherwise, you might as well run for your life.

We decided to try a frontal attack. We had worked out

a system of identification to distinguish friend from foe. We took old socks with us and each tied one round his sleeve. If we had paid for badges and armbands, we might have been reluctant to throw them away, but it was nothing to throw away an old sock if things got sticky and you wanted to melt back into the crowd.

We slowly gathered in the middle of the crowd, being very circumspect and clapping and cheering at the right moments. Finally, when we had a good wedge of about 50 all together at the front, we tied our socks on and charged, through the police cordon, through the others, and headed for the van. We managed to pull a few wires out and stop the speakers before it developed into a pitched battle. It didn't last long, barely a few minutes. About 40 were arrested, most of them bludgeoned down, then taken to hospital and arrested when they recovered.

Many escaped, like me, though we got a few thumps. I was off work for a week or two with a badly bruised shoulder; I couldn't move my arm. We demonstrated outside the court when our mates were sentenced. One got three months: he'd hit a policeman. And away went the judge and the newspapers again: "Red Revolution in the Land!" Everything was designed to protect the Fascists. I don't understand the thinking of the police, though I suspect they were brainwashed by the press propaganda. But the red revolutionaries they read about were very often just people from the synagogue down the road, or trades unionists.

We did actually manage to infiltrate some of the Fascists' indoor, all-ticket meetings. I remember a big one at the old Free Trade Hall. Unless you were a member of one of the Fascist groups, you had to apply to the BUF office for your free tickets. Since I wasn't known to them, that's what I did. The office was over a model shop on Corporation Street, close to Canon Street. On the top landing stood two huge blackshirt soldiers in jackboots, with silver flashes on their collars and black polished belts. After I had satisfied them that I was a normal Fascist-minded bloke, just wanting to attend the meeting, they let me into the office. It was like the third degree and everything was written down: where I worked, how long I had worked there, when and where I was born, a real thorough-going quiz. I heard later that some of my mates were refused tickets there and then, but they must have thought I was a fit person to listen to Mr Mosley, because I managed to get a ticket.

The ticket was numbered and I had to sit according to that number. That was made very clear. When me and my mates got inside on the night, we found that all the strangers who had applied for tickets were in one section. Very clever – a bit like the segregation of football fans nowadays. They knew that if trouble was going to break out, it would be in this section, because all the others were dyed-in-the-wool Fascists. So they could and did concentrate their patrols on us.

And it **was** patrolled. All the time the speakers were on, every couple of yards there were uniformed Fascists watching our section. You only needed to blow your nose, and you were out. When I say out, it was no polite request. They knew they were dealing with a potentially disruptive element, so even if a man was only whispering, or laughing in the wrong place, three or four thugs would converge, scattering the whole row to get at him if necessary, then physically haul him out. Once he was in the gangway, they banged him on the head with a truncheon to quieten him, then threw him to the floor and dragged him out by the heels.

It's a most unpleasant sensation. I know, because it happened to me at a meeting in Salford. I was dragged out but luckily my face was upwards. I'd been hit on the head and was unconscious, so didn't feel it. At the hospital it was found that the back of my neck was full of splinters from the rough plank floor over which they'd dragged me. It took a couple of hours to remove all those splinters. I suppose I was lucky not to be more seriously injured, because the thugs' grand finale would be to sling their victim up and out of the door like a sackful of rubbish. They did not care whether or not there were stone steps down to street level and there were many serious injuries.

When you were ejected from a Fascist meeting you were usually a hospital case, yet nobody was ever charged with assault. One chap nearly died in London. He was crippled for the rest of his life and after a lot of pressure in Parliament, the police made some sort of effort to investigate the assault. But it all came to nothing – they could not pin it on any one jackbooted thug. So the critics started accusing the party itself, but Mosley just waved any accusations away. It ended up with Conservative MPs answering the questions that were being asked, saying in effect that the injured man deserved all he got, for being an enemy of the state.

To get back to the Free Trade Hall meeting … I managed to stay to the end but I saw quite a few thrown out. It was a bad place to be thrown out of, the old Free Trade Hall, with lots of steps, a lot of dark corners, plus numerous little corridors and private rooms you could be dragged into, just to see you right before you were hurled down the stone steps. The pattern was always the same.

Whenever someone happened to shuffle his feet or otherwise draw attention to himself, the thugs would converge on him and a burst of cheering and clapping would come from the aficionados. This was to cover up the ejection, which would be fairly noisy, with boots going in, coshes flying and people shouting with pain.

One of the biggest Fascist meetings I can remember in Manchester was at Hulme Town Hall, in Stretford Road. Anti-Fascist demonstrators were not allowed to collect in crowds, so the technique was to stay in groups of about six or so and roam the side streets near the venue, or hide in corners until the inevitable procession. The Fascists would always de-bus a few streets away and then march to the meeting place. They were always highly-disciplined, to instil terror into the poor downtrodden peasants. And it was terrifying to watch, knowing they were there for one purpose only and that was to bash you. Seeing a marching group of 100 to 150 men, fully trained, as smartly uniformed as any soldier, certainly gave you something to think about.

Anyway, once they had entered the town hall, all its doors were closed and then the police ringed it, two or three deep. There was no chance of us getting in, but no one was inclined to go home and there were several thousand of us outside. Every side street was packed. In the street I was in, behind the hall, one group was singing 'The Red Flag' at the top of their voices. Our lot were singing 'Hallelujah I'm a Bum', and various other union and workers' songs. The police were trying to break us up, but they could not even force their way through. There were just too many of us; if I'd put my hands up above my head I couldn't have got them down again.

The meeting itself was well under way by this time.

170

But they had to come out eventually, so we decided to sabotage Mosley's getaway vehicle, a big, steel-sided van with wire mesh protecting all its glasswork from stones. We could not damage it, so somebody suggested turning it over. Everybody was shouting; the worst being the middle-aged and elderly Jewish women. Some of them had seen pogroms in Russia and Poland and knew what it was all about. God help anybody who had fallen into their hands. There would have been murder that night.

They were the ones, I think, who started to rock the van. It must have weighed about three tons, but there were scores of eager hands at work and the crowd all round was protecting them from the police baton charges. I had my hands on one of the tyres and we just kept on rocking away until eventually it crashed over. When Mosley came out with his bodyguard there was no van to take him away so he went back in, pretty quick! They stayed there all night.

All the rest of that night, the police kept busy, taking scores of demonstrators to the clink. It was a case of if you were there you were a criminal. I stayed until about 3am or 4am with my mates, practising guerrilla tactics. Being young we could run and we all knew the area well, so we kept on harassing the coppers by bobbing up where we were least expected, then disappearing down entries and over walls, nothing illegal, just jeering. It went on till daylight, and it was well into the morning before Mosley and his thugs got out of the town hall.

One incident that I was told about and would love to have seen, happened at a Fascist meeting on a croft near Strangeways jail. During the usual battle which ended the meeting, the jackboot thugs had split up and were running around in the crowd waving their bludgeons.

Two of them had chased a couple of lads I knew and one lad told me what happened next. They had managed to get a good few licks in at these thugs, which had so infuriated them that they had forgotten their usual cowardly caution and chased them down some side streets – right into the middle of a Jewish community!

Well, a bunch of middle-aged women got hold of these two jackbooted henchmen and tarred and feathered them – or the next best thing. Having completely stripped them, they then used whitewash brushes and yard brushes to cover them all over with thick black grease from a garage. Then they rolled them in sawdust, and chased them right back into the city. What a sight it must have been: two Fascist thugs running for their lives with about 30 screaming women chasing after them.

However, Mosley carried on undeterred and it was only the war that stopped him. He was building himself up to something big. If it hadn't been for the war I think he would have taken control of the country. It was so obvious that millions of pounds were being poured into his movement. The industrialists must have been backing him and he did just what they wanted, dividing the working people until there were more right wingers than left wingers. There were two main reasons for this, one being the aura of respectability that the Conservative Party cast over Mosley's followers, the other being the amount of fear generated by the jackboot army. A lot of people who would normally have been sympathetic, just were too afraid to stand up and be counted. You couldn't live in Wilmslow and be a Labour Party member. Well, you could, but you had to keep it very quiet.

This tight linking of social graces and respectability with political affiliation was very highly organised. It was quite blatant but all the media rested on it, films, stage and radio plays. And worst of all were the monthly magazines for women. There would be the gracious living bit in the middle pages, with the kitchen as big as a normal house. And practically all the good characters in the little stories that they put out for the happy housewife were the son of Lord Suchabody and the daughter of the local vicar or the bishop's niece, while the villains were always Labour Party members, trades union stewards, Reds.

So three quarters of the country was solidly indoctrinated. You had to be very careful what you said in company and stick with your own kind. The country was split. The wrong word could even get a man sacked. It happened to a pal of mine when we were working at Metro-Vicks [*Metropolitan-Vickers*] which later became GEC, in Trafford Park. I can't remember exactly what he said, but I think he called a charge hand a Conservative lackey or something equally innocuous.

I was brought in as a witness. They used a big office and it made a damned good courtroom. If it hadn't been for the tragedy, this bloke in danger of losing his job, it would have been one of the funniest things you ever saw, a really good scene for a play. The board of management sat at one end of a long table. The union steward was there, but in those days that didn't mean much because there were no closed shops. The chargehand had brought witnesses who weren't even there when it happened: a departmental manager, another chargehand and somebody else as a character witness.

It was conducted like a trial for murder! All it lacked was wigs and robes, and it went on for about two hours. I nearly put my foot in it. I was treating it as a joke because it was so unbelievable. They asked me, "Did he say this?"

"I don't know, he wasn't talking to me," I replied.

"Well," they said, "you must have heard him."

"Of course I heard him, but it didn't register."

Then I launched into a nonsensical diatribe about the function of the human brain and the selectiveness of the human ear which hears sounds, but does not register those you do not want to hear. A scientific explanation – sort of.

Well, this apparently made me a hostile witness and I was told to stand down. And after a lot more of this silly nonsense they decided the case would be settled if my mate apologised to the chargehand. So he did. A fortnight later he got the sack. And about a month later, so did I.

I have always said I was never into politics, but I certainly lived amongst politics. I never saw the whole picture, because only the intellectual who stands at the back and reads the books ever sees the whole picture. The bloke at the front getting his ribs kicked in sees nothing except the bloke who is kicking him.

But I certainly learned that there were two sides to politics.

CROSS-CHANNEL

CHAPTER 21

DUTCH TREATS

IN 1933, I decided to see what it was like on the Continent. Now at this period, a working man on the Continent was unheard of, unless he'd gone there to work. Most travellers were either people of means, or teachers, whose pay then must have been proportionally much higher than it is today. For an ordinary working bloke like me, it just wasn't on. There was nothing like the modern package tour – no special cheap trips. The Cooks Tour was just about beginning, but you still needed money. It was far out of my province.

However, when I was in work, I used to live as though as I was out of work and save every ha'penny. Then, if and when I came out of work, which was reasonably often, I would take off with this money and live as long as I could with it. What with Youth Hostelling, and various other expedients, I could live very cheaply.

But could I do as well across the Channel? I could but try. I got myself to Harwich, stayed there a couple of nights and haunted the waterside pubs. And by judicious inquiries, found a purser from an English cargo boat, who, for a couple of quid, agreed to get me across to Amsterdam. I had to more or less sign on as his assistant, which meant I did all the dirty work, as usual. But it was only for about eight or nine hours and we were across and that was the end of it.

At that stage I hadn't even had the sense to equip myself with an English-Dutch phrase book, or a map. I just landed in Amsterdam, with a few spare clothes. On Salford Docks I'd talked to seamen who'd been in Holland and Belgium, so, taking their advice, I looked for a cafe that said English Spoken. In the first two or three this was limited to the ordering of drinks and meals, but eventually I found a girl behind a counter who could at least maintain a simple conversation.

Englishmen at that time were regarded as the Yanks were later – everyone was held to be rich. I persuaded this girl that I was just an ordinary bloke, who worked in a factory, hadn't much money, and that I wanted somewhere to live very cheaply, preferably among people who could understand English, until I'd gained a slight command of Dutch.

She told me to hang about for an hour, and introduced me to another girl. She also worked in Amsterdam, lived just outside Volendam and came in for a drink and a snack before her train home. She spoke English and after hearing my story said right away: "Come home with me. My mother will look after you until you get settled somewhere."

It was like being back home. The Dutch are very much like Lancashire folk. The house was just outside Volendam, which since the war has become something of a tourist haunt. Some older people still wore the old costume then – wooden clogs, baggy trousers, little lace three-piece hats – but they wore them naturally, not as a gimmick.

This girl's mother was kindness itself. From the very start she treated me as part of the family. It was embarrassing. They wouldn't let me pay. Their son was the skipper of a fishing trawler and he was at sea when I arrived. "You can use his room," they said. "No good it being empty when you need somewhere to sleep."

It seemed the villagers had never met a real English working chap, who had spent all his life in factories and mills just as they had. Everybody wanted to talk to me. I sat for many an hour on street benches, talking to children and their teachers, who wanted to practise their English. I'd be invited into a cafe for a drink and there would be whole tables full of men and lads watching me like hawks, making sure I didn't spend any of my own money. Even if I went in alone, the man or woman behind the counter would take no money, saying my presence was enough. I brought custom in, it seemed.

And all they wanted to do was talk about work and about ordinary people. The English sailors they had met in Amsterdam weren't prepared to sit down and talk about their life in England. Sailors were too busy doing other things! The men wanted to know about life in the industrial north, and the girls wanted to know what kind of clothes English working girls wore, what they did at night, what were their relationships with their parents. I did my best, but there were lots of questions I couldn't answer properly. I had a marvellous time during the four months I was there.

After about a month the son came home for a week, and do you know, he wouldn't let me move out of his bedroom! He slept downstairs on a hard, old-fashioned settle, all wooden slats and a few cushions. Then he said, "Do you want to earn some money? How would you like to sail?" "Oh," I said, "I'm no sailor." But he persuaded me to go back out to sea with him. There were only six of us. I was assistant cook, but I found that on a fishing boat, it doesn't matter what your title is, when it's time to fish everybody gets on to the nets. I didn't know this. I also didn't know that when your hands are wet through and you're handling rough nets, you get cut to pieces until you've grown the requisite segs and calluses.

I was to get a half share in the catch. The skipper got two shares, each seaman got one share, and I got half a seaman's share because I was not a regular crew member. Even so, it would be a fair amount. The sea wasn't too bad, but I still felt rotten all the time. And whenever it got a little bit rough I got really sick. I'm no seaman.

But it was the pudding that put the top hat on it! We'd made a big milk pudding, about two gallons of it, in a big enamel bowl. The two of us wrestled it on to the deck just outside the galley to cool down. As we got on with preparing the rest of the evening meal, the ship's little white dog, which they kept to control the rats, came trotting past. It sniffed at the pudding, burned its nose, yelped, and then piddled in it! "Hey!" I said to the cook. "Look there! Look what's happened!"

"Never mind," he said. "Stir it up, nobody know."

So I stirred it up with a big wooden spoon and nobody seemed to notice it. But for the rest of the trip I lived off bread and tinned meat and stuff I'd cooked myself. It was about three weeks before we returned to Amsterdam, long enough to cure me. I never could have been a sailor. I can get sick rowing a boat on a park lake.

Later, the skipper's sister, who worked in a market garden office in Amsterdam, got me a temporary job there. A chap who checked the vans and wagons as they were loaded with bulbs for export, had had an accident and was going to be off a couple of weeks. All I had to do was tick a list and write down some details on a manifest, as the stuff was loaded; a really easy, comfortable job, and those I worked with were a pleasant set of people.

The girl also used to take me to a cafe at dinnertime. She had a set of Amsterdam friends and once we stayed late with them and had a really wild night out. Good job her mother thought we'd gone to the pictures! After the party I stayed late several more times, having nights out with lads I'd palled up with at the works. But the girl's mother, I found, was worrying about me. She thought the big city would corrupt me. And the girl was getting a bit moody. She was sort of basking in the glory of having the English boy living at her house and my staying on in Amsterdam and getting later trains home was taking some of the shine off it.

And then the job ended, I was back again in Volendam and everything was all right, except that I was beginning to get bored. I was doing odd jobs around the house, helping to cook and clean. In a Dutch house, most waking time seemed to be spent cleaning. Inside every house that I entered was a vestibule lined with shelves for outdoor shoes. If you wanted to clean them, all the cleaning tackle was there too. And that was where you would change into slippers. There were several pairs in various sizes for visitors, but if nothing would fit, you would enter in stockinged feet.

But I was getting bored, just stooging around the village, waiting for evening when everybody would be back from work. Then I started saying hello to a bonny young girl outside one of the shops. She knew about as much English as I knew Dutch, but with help from a lad of about twelve, who had passable English, I found that she helped at a special camp about a mile and a half outside the village.

The camp had big heavy English-type bell-tents, the sort used in the First World War, about eight or nine staff and about 40 young lads and girls, aged between eight and thirteen. All were what we would now call problem children. Not criminal, recalcitrant more than anything. Some were too much for their parents and some were difficult in school. So they sent them to this camp for a fortnight.

There was no punishment; it was a free and open camp, with activities they could join if they wished and sing-songs at night. Everything was open. They just had to obey normal camp rules about litter and observe meal and bed times. It was claimed that it did these youngsters a lot of good, just living together. They'd been used to getting all their own way and most had never been subjected to discipline.

At the camp, if you wanted to do something and the bloke next to you didn't like it, it was a case of who was the bigger. So they would fight and scratch, boys and girls alike and the staff would leave them to it. Then they would quietly take the winner to one side and say, "Well, now you're the cock of the camp ... try and beat us!" In other words, they still had to conform to the rules of the camp. And it worked. The youngsters became a lot more amenable to discipline, realising that if you're going to live amongst people, you've got to have some rules for living.

It impressed me. I ended up going there for several hours, nearly every day. I got on well with the youngsters, mainly, I suppose, because I had once been a bit like them in temperament, a bit of a rebel. I taught them woodcraft, the stuff I'd learned in the Scouts. We used to lay trails through the woods and hunt for one another. I taught them conjuring tricks and how to cook.

I taught them Indian lore, how to make cooking fires and counsel fires and leave no trace of either.

I got into a bit of trouble when I taught them how to make moccasins and they cut up two blankets to get the material! But at the end of my five weeks of helping, the Dutch education people gave me a certificate, commending me for my voluntary effort. It had had good results, they said, and some of the things I had started would be kept on.

All very ego-boosting, of course, but I wasn't as successful with the girl. While we got on well with the youngsters and around the camp, that was about as far as it went. I found Dutch girls were very … well … difficult.

I also became involved with the church. The rector asked me to go to a social evening and give a talk to some older people about life in England. He meant church life, but I never was a churchgoer and had to disguise the fact that I was more or less an atheist. I had vague memories of going to Sunday school, mainly because my mother wanted me out of the way while she got the dinner ready. And I was taken to a few Sunday evenings at a Baptist church in Nelson when I was about eight, by a bloke who lived next door.

So I could bluff it through for my Dutch audience, but within the first couple of minutes, on the few occasions I did it, I would turn the subject to something I did know about. I remember talking all one night about witchcraft and Pendle Hill, which I knew backwards, having spent much of my childhood days climbing up and down it. They were fascinated by the idea of witches on a mountain. Anything to do with mountains fascinates the Dutch, with their own land being so flat.

It did me a lot of good. I got to know practically

everybody in the village. Everybody used to smile and nod. Nearly three and a half months I stayed there. I could have stayed for ever. But I decided that home is best and when I told everybody I was leaving, some old ladies were actually weeping. They nearly persuaded me to stay. But I'm a drifter at heart. When I left, practically the whole village came to the station, pushing parcels on me, presents, bunches of flowers. Oh dear! I needed a handcart to move all the stuff they gave me. I had to give most of it away on the station at Amsterdam, because most of the parcels contained food. But the parson's gift was a wristwatch, inscribed inside. I lost it during the war. I was very sorry to leave and swore I'd go back. I told everybody I would come back next year for a week or two, but somehow it never worked out.

In later years, reading some of the wartime escape stories, I had no difficulty understanding the enormous sacrifices that the Dutch people made to help British soldiers and others to escape, even being murdered by the Germans for doing so. The Dutch are like that.

CHAPTER 22

GERMAN LESSONS

THE FOLLOWING year, 1934, I decided to have a look at Spain and ended up somewhere else entirely. With my usual lack of planning, I got down to Southampton and this time had to pay to get across to Le Havre. In a cafe there I bought a couple of butties and a glass of wine. I had enough French to do that and enough fingers. It's a good system, finger language.

Anyway, I was sitting outside this cafe and who should come along but Stan, a bloke who lived just down the street from me. He had never told me this previously, but apparently, after a successful career as an amateur welterweight boxer, he'd run a boxing booth in Paris for about a year. It flopped, so he had started another in Brussels. That eventually failed too, so he had returned to England.

Now he was off for a week's holiday in Paris with his wife. "Come with us," he said, "and I'll show you a Paris you never knew existed. You can go on your jaunt afterwards." So I did. He'd brought his car over and it saved me from having to walk. The week in Paris was alright, but it didn't really suit my temperament. I'm a gutter merchant at heart – I like to mooch around back alleyways in working class districts, going in little cafes and talking to ordinary people.

With Stan's connections, I met a lot of fairground show-people along the Rue de Rivoli, where there were all sorts of little penny-catcher shows, something like the

Golden Mile at Blackpool, only more elaborate. I remember one bloke showing me exactly how his particular illusion worked, with mirrors, darkness and kidology. You seemed to be in a dark sort of garden, with flowers everywhere, and when you had looked your fill, they faded away and the scene reappeared, but this time covered in snow. Very effective.

One day we were sitting in a cafe when more people seemed to be passing than usual. It turned out there was to be an execution outside the Santé Prison; they used to guillotine them in public then. I wasn't keen, but Stan wanted to go. His missus went back to their hotel for a lie-down and we set off for the Santé, but it was all over by the time we got there and they were swilling the blood away and stripping the guillotine. The blade had already gone and the woodwork was being dismantled and put on to carts and trundled back into the prison. I was glad. I had no desire to see a bloke get his head chopped off.

Anyway, I got to know Paris, as I did a fair bit of stooging around. After the war, I went there quite often, and got to know Paris almost as well as I know Manchester. But with a couple who only wanted to see tourist Paris, I didn't feel free at all. I enjoyed it, but when I'm with anybody, if I can't run away and leave them, I have this sense of being caged up. So when Stan and his wife went home on the Friday, I stayed over till Monday, reviewing my plans for going to Spain.

Problem was, there had been trouble there for a year or two, with the Basques battling a bit here and there. I'd planned to get down to Madrid by bus and on foot, via Hendaye, a place in southern France on the northern Spanish frontier. But then I would have had to go through Basque country. I was a bit wary of this, because bullets and bombs are no respecters of people.

So I decided to go to Germany instead. Off I went, bus and feet, got to Nancy, then worked my way down, mostly by train, from Stuttgart to Munich.

And there I had the chance to have a look at Hitler. The 'great man' wasn't all that great then, but Munich was his stamping ground. They had built a huge sports palace and he was to make an important speech there.

I applied at the tourist office for a ticket to hear him. I had to apply well in advance and it tied me to Munich for a week. When the time came, there were three other guests in the little hotel where I was staying who had also applied – a couple of Spaniards and a Danish fellow. We waited in the foyer and in marched a couple of Brownshirts, armed to the teeth with truncheons and revolvers.

They lined us up, marched us out to a big bus and took us to the arena. Once inside we had to walk. It seemed like miles and every step of the way more Brownshirts lined the corridors on both sides. Eventually, they took us up to a glass-walled room right at the top. We wouldn't have heard a sound up there, but Hitler's voice and the roar of the huge audience came booming in through big loud-speakers.

Even though you disagreed with it all, it was a very impressive sight. He certainly knew how to stir people's feelings. The amphitheatre was huge – more than twice the size of a football pitch. And it was crammed with Hitler Youth, Hitler Madchen. All the girls and boys, all the troops, Blackshirts, Brownshirts, bands and 60-foot long banners on poles, black and gold, black and red, like Roman legions.

Down in the amphitheatre, thousands of well-trained fanatics made patriotic patterns to the music, with coloured cards held above their heads. It was a marvellous sight, but difficult to see unless you were tall like me. The glass wall was in front of us and a row of Brownshirts stood with their backs to it, shoulder to shoulder, facing us with gun holsters unbuttoned. We had to peer over their shoulders.

The great little man, when he arrived, looked about as big as a match head from our viewpoint. We would have needed a nine-inch naval gun to hit him. Just a tiny speck and we didn't understand a word he said. Well, I didn't.

So that was my run-in with Hitler. When it was all over, they put us back on the bus and took us back to the hotel. They even put a guard on the hotel door to stop us going out until the streets had cleared. They didn't really want foreigners there at all. But having read about Hitler and seen bits of newsreels, I had to see him for myself; and having seen him, I'd had enough. For the sake of an hour and a half listening to this screeching maniac, I'd ruined a day. I'd have been better off moving on. And as soon as I could, that's what I did.

I headed for Austria, intending to go through the Schwarzwald, the Black Forest, and on to Vienna. But somehow or other I got side-tracked and found myself in Innsbruck. I stayed in a guest house, a favourite drinking place for local university students. I became friends with some of them and when I talked about climbing in England, they asked me to join them on a climbing trip in Switzerland. They even offered to lend me the correct gear, but the trip was not till a month later, so I said I would try and get back to go with them.

I moved on, following the River Inn, to where it meets the Danube near Linz. This time I was in a youth hostel, up in the forest. And that was where I managed to wave the Union Jack for the first time.

English youth hostels were free and easy, but with a certain camaraderie. At this time and in this part of Europe, however, most of the walking was done by the Wander Vogel, the Wander birds, and these were the Hitler Youth, the Hitler Jung, a pretty poisonous bunch.

I was in a hostel near Linz, carrying my meal from the kitchen into the dining room, when in marched a whole bunch of these Wander Vogels, led by a smartly uniformed chap aged about 20. The others were in shorts, but it was like a uniform too, the way they wore it. In they marched. Halt! They all lined up. Everything was military, and I thought, "So this is what it's all about. This is what I've read about."

I never found out their leader's name, for which I'm rather grateful. We were eating at long tables, with long wooden benches. And he sat there, making snide remarks at me with his half dozen words of English, mainly about me being degenerate. He had been conditioned to think that everybody who wasn't German and in the Hitler Youth was no good. It began to niggle me. I kept dodging out of his way but he kept following me and everything I tried to do he would be there, sneering. So I began to cast about for ways of dealing with him. I daren't say or do anything. It had to be a cunning sort of move.

I knew I could out-walk anything on two feet in that hostel. So I agreed with him that the English were degenerate weaklings given to boasting, all the things that they were taught in the schools in fact, just as we were taught that the French ate frogs and the Spanish lived on olive oil. Then, towards the end of the evening, I said to him, "Could I walk with you tomorrow, so that you can show me, how you do it? I'd be glad to learn."

After a lot of palaver he agreed, but added, "You fall out, we leave you!"

"Yes, that's all right," I replied. "Where are you going?"

I think he said about eight or ten kilometres, to the next hostel. Not far at all. I used to do that before breakfast. That's not a joke. I've done eight kilometres between six o'clock in the morning and half-past nine, just to get to somewhere in particular.

So I set off with them in the morning, and I kept having discussions with him about the map, enough to confuse him, to make him not quite sure where he was. And eventually I led them all into a bog. Wet socks – the finest thing in the world for making blisters. Meanwhile, I kept niggling on about the map and managed to get them well and truly lost. And it turned out I was the only one with a compass and probably the only one there who knew how to use one. Their leader certainly had no idea. He was just what he'd been accusing me of – all mouth.

Instead of eight kilometres, I made sure they did about 22. They kept stopping for a rest in the end, which is fatal when you are blistered and stiff, because every time you sit down you get up sorer and stiffer than ever. We nearly didn't reach the hostel, and when we did, instead of 5pm, it was turned 10pm. They'd missed the evening meal, but the kitchen staff gave them something. They sat around; rubbing boracic and spirit on to the blisters and liniment on to their legs and shoulders.

Meanwhile, I organised a midnight hike, explaining that it was a lot more interesting to find your way in the dark, returning at first light. They didn't dare lose face and say no. I don't know how far we went – another good few kilometres. But in the morning they just sat there.

They'd given up. They were going to rest for the day.

Their leader was silent, surly and scowling. "Well," I said, "I'm sorry you couldn't make it. I was going to see whether you were willing to come along with me today." I told him I was going to a place about 20 kilometres away. He never spoke a word. I expected to be put up against a wall and shot, but I never saw him again.

Silly really, but I was proud of that little episode. And it wasn't the last. At another hostel, not far from Vienna, another bunch of Hitler Youth arrived. These were fitter – physical culture fanatics – getting up early in the morning and doing knee-bends, skipping, and club swinging. A couple took it upon themselves to teach me. They were doing the basic movements: one arm stuff, swinging it behind and mind you don't knock the back of your head off.

I had done hours and hours of club swinging and could do all sorts of fancy tricks with a pair of four-pound clubs. But these big-heads didn't know that. Eventually, they gave me a second club and I did the basic two-arm movement for a while. Then I said, "Does it work when you do this?" and started doing all the fancy double twists and alternates. You should have seen their faces!

The next thing was, they were going to do a bit of boxing. Oh, dear! They picked on all the things that I knew about. I weighed just over ten stone then and their leader was the nearest to my weight, perhaps three pounds heavier. "Do you know of this box-fighting?" he asked. "Well," I said, "it looks easy enough." Eventually, he enticed me into a ring they'd marked out with stones on a lawn behind an old castle. For a couple of rounds, we just sparred and I thought, "We'll stick at this … he's not a bad lad for a Nazi. I'll leave him alone." I wasn't even worried about the way the kid with the watch was timing the rounds, letting them go on if his chief seemed to be winning and stopping them short if he didn't.

But then, around the beginning of the fifth round, I was rubbing my gloves on my shorts, when he let me have one right between the eyes. Oh, it was a cracker. Knocked me flat on my back. "That's it, mate!" I thought. "You've definitely filled your sheet in there." I got up and gave him a pasting, probably the best he'd ever had. I didn't try to knock him out, but he certainly knew he'd been box-fighting. He had plenty of bruises and red spots when he decided to call it a draw.

Later that evening he came to me in the common room and apologised. "I think you try to kid me," he said.

"You're right, I did." But I apologised too, qualifying it by saying, "Don't go around thinking that everybody who is not a German is no good, because there are a lot of people in all parts of the world who are just as good as a German and like me they will be pleased to demonstrate it, if you want to start anything."

I must have been foreseeing the war.

CHAPTER 23

VIENNA TO MUNICH

I WAS planning my route to Vienna when two Austrian blokes I'd met in the hostel at Linz offered me a lift in their canvas canoe down the Danube. They had a spare seat. I had never realised the vastness of that river. In some parts it's the best part of three-quarters of a mile wide and like a mill race in others. They float huge log rafts down it. And it isn't blue. Old Strauss should have been summoned under the Trade Descriptions Act. It's a dirty brown, the sort of colour you flush down the toilet.

Going down-river, as we were, was largely a matter of maintaining steerage, just keeping away from the banks, staying clear of other boats and the log rafts and keeping head on to the river. Not really hard work, but the sheer concentration is tiring when you're being whirled along at least as fast as a Manchester bus.

Once in Vienna I stayed in a little guest house. They didn't serve meals but in the hallway was a door that led into the cafe next door. The cash desk girl was learning English, so I got all my meals free, plus a ready-made guide and adviser. "If ever you get lost within Vienna's walls," she said, "picture it as a wheel. The streets radiate outwards like spokes, from the Stadthaus to the Gurtel wall, which forms the rim. All you have to do is get on the Gurtel and walk round … mind you, it's about four miles round … until you come to the street you want."

A couple of days later, in the early afternoon, I was somewhere near the centre, having a beer, when a

Cook's tour crocodile came by, all in twos, a leader at the front and a whipper-in bringing up the rear to see that nobody strayed. And there in the middle were two lads from Nottingham University whom I'd met in various English youth hostels. "Wait there," they shouted, "we're coming back!"

They told the leader they wanted to break away and he came back to check whether I knew my way about. "Know my way about? I know every back alley in Vienna! Give over!" So they broke free and we wandered from cafe to cafe, getting steadily stinko. By 9pm we'd had nothing to eat and none of us was in a fit state to be out. We were really piddled. "Right," they said, "our hotel's on something strasse. How do we get there?"

"Leave it to me," said confident Graney, "I'll get you there."

I took them on to the Gurtel. We wandered along, having more little sips here and there, schnapps, gin, various beers. After an hour or so, one lad asked, "Where are we going? We've passed this place before, we had a drink here."

"No, no," I said. "You're just drunk, mate."

Round we went again, me more or less carrying them by this time, one arm of each around my neck. No sign of it. At midnight we gave up and sat on a bench till a policeman came by. He put us in a taxi and within two minutes the taxi driver had dropped them off. We could have walked it in about three minutes! Then he ran me to my place and I had to pay the lot, which I couldn't really afford.

"Oh dear!" said the girl the next day. "I should have told you. Some of the streets start out with one name, go through a square and come out of it with a different name!" I lost my reputation with those lads. They spread the word around the English youth hostels: "Never let Paul Graney be your guide in Vienna!"

Two days out of Vienna, I met two German brothers who were just finishing a holiday. They lived in Munich and said, "If you get anywhere near Munich you must come and stay with us a day or two and we'll show you around." So I did, and they couldn't do enough for me.

They were in the Hitler Youth. They didn't like it, but they had to be in it. Like many Germans, they agreed with some of the things Hitler was doing but they didn't like all the military emphasis, such as the beautiful autobahns, which were designed chiefly to move troops and equipment more efficiently.

We were out having a drink once when one of them said: "What would you do, Paul, if there was a war, and you had a rifle and you pointed it at a German soldier and it turned out to be me?"

"Well," I said, "I'm a pacifist by profession. I don't believe in wars of any sort. I would try not to have a rifle in my hand or be wearing a uniform, but I know when wars start it's nearly impossible to avoid them. But if I saw somebody I knew, I would lift the sights up a bit and shoot a few yards over him, making sure I missed him. The only trouble is, could I trust him to do the same? You see, in a war, you often have to become a murderer, just to survive."

We didn't pursue it further, but I've often thought about that dilemma, and I'm certain that I would have fired over him. Nobody would have known.

We had one or two spots of bother in Munich, which was the real hotbed of Nazism. I was obviously a foreigner, by the cut of my clothes, and once or twice, even in daylight, we were jostled and pushed and called names. The two lads had to face it as well, just for being with me.

But it was worse at night, when all the Brownshirt boys and Hitler Youths had been out supping and were roaming the streets in gangs. The worst of it was that they were encouraged to do it. The police looked the other way. So my two pals lent me a pair of shorts, a military style jacket with a swastika armband and a peaked cap. While I had these on, as long as I kept my mouth shut, I was all right.

As it turned out, they never bothered us. I kept my eyes open and saw quite a few things that were typical of their mindlessness. Goebbels [*the German Propaganda Minister*] had put the word out to, "Smash the Jews." So these young thugs would go to a Jewish shop, scrawl 'Jews' in whitewash across the window, then smash it.

Then there was the book-burning. There were a lot of proscribed books and it was quite in order for them to go into libraries, colleges, schools and shops and have themselves a wonderful bonfire. One night I saw them smash a bookshop window. Half a dozen were sorting out what to burn. But when the fire started burning a bit low, they slung every book in the shop on it! Even Hitler's own *Mein Kampf*. They just wanted a blaze.

I didn't wave the Union Jack in Munich. Oh dear no. One night, quite late, we were making for home in pouring rain when we came across three drunken thugs who had caught hold of an old woman. She was obviously not very heavy and they were just throwing her from one to the other. She was sobbing and weeping. I stopped and the two lads got hold of me, one to each arm, "Come on, don't get mixed up in it. Even to stop and look is enough to get you the same treatment." They were frightened to death. When I turned at the corner to look back, the old lady was on the ground and Hitler's young pride were busy tearing her coat off. What happened to her, I don't know.

A lot of people were killed on the streets. It was mindless and terrifying. If they shouted "Stop!" and you ran, they would shoot at you. And no one had guns except these thugs. Anyone could be caught up in it. It was enough just to be there. I soon learned to make myself scarce, but even that could bring trouble. If you were in a bierkeller and three or four of these blokes came in looking for trouble and you got up and walked out, you'd insulted them.

They would puff out their manly chests and stand in front of you, demanding to know where you were going and why. If you didn't give a satisfactory answer you could count on getting a good thumping. It was hell on earth. No wonder nine-tenths of the German population were in the Nazi Party. They had to agree with it, just to keep their feet on their own hearth.

In the early days of the concentration camps, there were more so-called racially pure Germans held as political prisoners than there were Jews. They'd call for you in the middle of the night, without speaking a word, force you to get dressed, then bundle you into a car. Your relatives could make all the inquiries they liked. Nobody knew where you'd gone. And you never came home.

That's how it was when I was there. I never went back to Germany, I'd had enough.

TIME OUT

CHAPTER 24

THAT SPORTING LIFE

LIFE was not all graft and misery. As you have just seen, a determined ordinary chap could see a fair bit of the world. And although up to now I have concentrated mainly on subjects to do with work, or the lack of it, interwoven with all those episodes were periods when you could more or less do what you wanted. When you were not working or looking for work, there was a space in time in which you could, quite literally, please yourself, within the limitations of your finances, of course, and of your station in life.

My earliest leisure time of any importance was in 1924 when I came to Manchester. In Nelson I had been more or less a country boy, living only a street away from the fields and woods, Pendle Hill only a short walk away. So Manchester was totally new and rather daunting. It was not long, though, before I found the answer. I had made friends with a lad from Hulme, Harold Nolan. He was in the Scouts and very soon I joined him, in the Third Salford St Cyprians.

I lived in a rough area of Salford and whether I was there, or in Hulme with Harold, we found that if we mentioned Scouts, we were sneered at. But that scouting experience proved to be the groundwork for the rest of my life. First, it taught me how to survive; how to camp out and live off the country; how to stay dry and warm. It has been very useful, not only in my on-the-road days, but in wartime too. I was also taught to look after myself. Not the pure in thought, word and deed thing, but physically; to be able to stand on my own feet. I learned the rudiments of boxing, a bit of wrestling, enough to give me a sort of confidence. At that age it was a cocky sort of teenage confidence, but backed up by even a rudimentary ability, it wasn't so bad. At least I could walk down a street and if people said anything to me, I knew that I was on the best side. Usually.

An ex-Navy man gave us Master at Arms Badge training: fencing, single stick and quarter staff, not to be proficient at it but enough to look after ourselves. It has certainly got me out of many a scrape since and probably even saved my life more than once. It also conditioned my thinking for the rest of my life. It made me confident. Even today, when I'm old and falling apart, with no more ability to look after myself than a tiny baby, I've still retained the social confidence I had then. I'm not afraid to go anywhere.

During the war years, in the army, where a stick is no use against a bullet, I still had this confidence. On one occasion my officer called it a lack of fear. It wasn't. I was as frightened as everybody else. I had to wash my pants out more than once, but when you know you are as capable as any other man, you grow this air of confidence. You can stand up to people and you never lose it.

We did not stay with scouting much after our sixteenth birthdays; by then we were fully occupied running a football club. We had no money. Most of us were out of work and of those working most got only coppers in spending money. I remember just how it started. It would be about the end of 1924 and Harold Nolan and I were at a loose end, walking around the Silver Street/Queen Street/Hargreave Street part of Hulme, a rough area where every corner had a gambling school and the coppers walked in threes.

We were just chatting and suddenly it clicked. We rounded up another nine who wanted to play football and without any money or previous knowledge, we applied for admission to the Moss Side and District League, as the Hulme Albion Football Club. There were three or four leagues in this association, based mainly on age and we put in for one where the average age of the players was supposed to be 16. It meant that if you had a lad of ten playing for you, you could also have a bloke of 22, which led to some very odd-looking line-ups! We had to find the £1 entrance fee first, then two shillings and sixpence a week referee's fees. Then we had to find a ground. The first we applied for was out at Stretford, a farmer's field. I forget exactly what he wanted, but to us it was astronomical – £5 or £6 a season. Hopeless.

So we applied to the corporation and eventually got a ground on St George's Park. We knew it as The Barracks. The story went that it was where the Manchester Militia were stationed at the time of the Peterloo massacre. But now it was a recreation ground, with steel pipe goal posts which broke your shoulder if you ran into them. It had no turf, just red shale. I can't see much in my knees, but after more than 50 years I've still got some of that shale embedded in my elbows.

So, there we were. Somehow we had to pay for all this. It was not very much, but we didn't have the price of a cinema seat between us. But my mate Harold was a bit of a financial genius, and he came up with a good wheeze. We went to a little shop in Hargreave Street, just an ordinary house with a few things on show in the window. The old lady who ran it supplied all the local people, usually 'on tick', to pull them through the bad times. She knew us all and we knew her. And we asked her: "Would you make up a five-shilling grocery parcel and put it in your window and we'll make out a raffle prize label for it? As soon as we've collected five shillings, we'll give it to you and you don't need to part with it until we've paid you."

Bless her soul, she did it for us. One of the lads borrowed his little brother's John Bull printing outfit, and we got a couple of tuppenny books of 1-to-100 cloakroom tickets and stamped Hulme Albion Football Club on the back of every one. It was highly illegal to run a raffle, but we did it, and we made about ten shillings the first week – halfway towards the association fee.

But there was another problem: we were not allowed to play unless we were at least in matching jerseys and wore proper football boots. You couldn't go on wearing a pair of big hobnailed army boots, though they would allow one or two to play in trousers if they didn't have shorts. They knew the difficulties with money, these people, but they wanted to keep the thing more or less orthodox. In the end my mother provided the shorts. Twelve pairs to start with and all made to measure, which was unusual. She got the cloth from the mill where she worked and in her younger days she had been a seamstress. We borrowed a set of jerseys from Hulme Celtic, a team which had been operating for some time.

Then we had to buy a new ball about once a month – quite an item at 15 shillings to £1 a time. Anyway, somehow or other we got started on our first season, struggling, borrowing and cadging money. One lad got a spare time job on the market, pushing a barrow. Dodgy, because he was signing on the dole and if they'd found out he would probably have been prosecuted and certainly kicked off the dole. Other lads sold things. I know one fellow sold his bike for twelve shillings so we could pay some fee or other.

The following summer, a bloke who ran a coal-yard just behind Hulme Church in Corbett Street said we could use the big empty room over his office for a meeting place. "I'll charge you rent when you've got some money together," he said.

It was an enormous room, bare-boarded and full of coal dust. But it was better than a Christmas present! We got stuck into cleaning it, with some of the lads' sisters helping, with scrubbing brushes and mops, plus paint, distemper and whitewash that we had scrounged. It was going to be our evening club, a sort of youth club, if you like. We made a canteen counter in one corner, with shelves and cupboards made of old wooden cases from the Maypole grocers.

We decided we'd have it green, but we'd no money to buy green distemper. We only had cheap whitewash. But at that time there was what they called raddle, which came in red or green. It was a sort of soluble stone, like the donkey stones you did the front steps with, except that this was mainly used for hearth stones. My mother used to do ours green. Every week as we polished the fire irons and the brasswork, she would rub a piece of wet cloth over the hearthstone, rub the green stone over the hearth, then the wet cloth again and it all came green. And this was the stuff we dissolved in our whitewash to make green distemper. Where there's a will!

When it came time to make partitions, tables and benches, we did what everybody else did – tramped to Trafford Park, to the early Ford factory, where stuff was delivered in enormous packing cases, some nearly as big as houses. Lots of people bought them or pinched them to make garden sheds and hen huts. Up in the hills near Glossop there was a complete bungalow made of them. We couldn't nick whole boxes, but late at night we could get away with loose boards the unpackers had left lying around. These were about three quarters of an inch thick, seven inches wide and anything from four to twelve feet long. Then we would carry them back to Hulme down all the back streets and along the Bridgewater canal bank in the middle of the night. And so we built the Hulme Albion Football Club.

But we still needed money. So we started a £2 to a penny stunt, based on football. Again it was a matter of Sunday working. The whole gang, anything up to 20 of us, would sit in the clubroom, using John Bull outfits to stamp hundreds of combinations of teams on paper tickets. Each ticket cost a penny and the highest total score won £2, with a £1 second prize. We even evolved a special way of folding the tickets so they could not be looked at. It took us weeks to work it all out. Then, on a Sunday after the gymnasium session (we had a gym going by then) 30 or so lads and girls (the blokes' sisters and their friends) would take the tickets out to sell. We made a good few pounds a week on the scheme. It made us solvent.

Then came the pie and peas affair. We had started selling snacks and cups of tea in our little canteen. A fair amount of food was also sold in the streets in those days and one summer evening, when we had all the windows open, a beautiful pie and peas cart stopped outside. It was pulled by a pony and had three highly polished brass boilers with chimneys. One sold hot pies and the other two sold black or green peas.

For peas, if you took your own basin, he would fill it for a penny. And his pies were marvellous. We started getting them in for the canteen. They were the best I had ever tasted and because we bought two or three dozen, he let us have them for tuppence each instead of threepence. I can still remember the taste. We would wait at the open windows and all shoot down to the street. The canteen staff would go with a box to get the wholesale ones and the rest of us the hot ones. They really were gradely. We even got a stock of small enamel basins and cheap aluminium spoons for the peas. Things went well for six or seven months, but then we didn't see the bloke for about a month. Then we read in the paper that he had been sent to jail. He was making his pies out of cats and dogs! He was paying kids a tanner for a cat and ninepence for a dog. I don't think I ate another pie for about four years after that.

As well as selling coal, the bloke who owned the yard hired out barrel organs. So when we decided to start Saturday night dances, radio being very much in its infancy and gramophones not as prolific as they are now, we rigged up a block and tackle to hoist one of these barrel organs through a big trap door in the floor of our club room. The 'band leader' was the bloke who turned the handle all night, usually me because I couldn't dance.

I wonder what modern youngsters would think of things like this? Yet we had a ferocious pride in what we had achieved. Everybody had worked at it and respected it. You didn't dare throw a toffee paper on the floor in that club because the bloke whose turn it was to sweep up would be round after you and belt you over the head with the brush: "Oi! I'm sweeping here! Stop littering it up."

It wasn't all socialising. Three nights a week were set aside for training when the girls weren't allowed in. Club swinging was popular. I've spent hours swinging clubs and skipping. Eventually we obtained the services of a chap named Boy McCormick, a big fellow who had been a contender for the world heavyweight championship, one of the best-known boxers in England in his day, but he had ended up punch-drunk, all his co-ordination gone. He used to shamble along, twitching and wobbling and he couldn't speak very well. But he had just finished a series of silent films called *The Corinthians*, two-reelers about the famous men of the bare knuckle days. That was when Boy McCormick had started, in the last century. So to us he had glamour – the aura of a film star.

We had built a training ring, and he started to teach us to box. That was a time! I could never convince my mother, when I came home with thick lips, black eyes or a busted nose, that it was only friendly. "Only practising," she'd say, "and they're hitting you on the nose like that!"

Boxing was just coming up in Manchester then. It didn't really arrive until the era of the world champion, Jackie Brown. In my teenage years, there were just one or two boxing booths and several boxing clubs which put on a show about once a month. In Stretford Road, not far from our club, was a broken-English-speaking barber called Frank Gotz, who traded on the similarity between his own name and that of world champion wrestler, Frank Gotch. The barber had a room like ours, over a coal-yard, where he promoted alternate weekly bouts of wrestling and boxing and one way or another he managed to fix up a night when three from our club were matched with three from another.

I was our welterweight. I weighed about 10 stone 11 pounds. Then there was a lightweight and a chap about my weight, Jimmy Smith. It would be half a crown for each winner and 'nowt' for the loser. It was fame to us, was that, to go in a ring with a chance of being paid for it. Old McCormick started training us, trying to teach us how the professionals went on, which was a daft thing to do, as we'd only be fighting young lads like ourselves.

My fight was against a bloke nicknamed Battling Chuckapenny. He used to dodge and duck about, a bit like Ali, always dancing and shuffling. He never tried to hit you until he saw an opportunity, and then he would come round with an overarm smash on the top of your head. It would knock you to your knees, that thump, and I'd had one or two before I managed to hit him hard enough to make him give up. I had a headache for a month and Î told McCormick I'd had enough. You can learn how to ride with a left or brush it off, pull your stomach in from a hook and keep your head back from a cross punch, but this Chuckapenny business, oh, no!

Anyway, a few weeks later this Gotz fellow decided to stage a battle royal. None of us had ever heard of it, but old McCormick said they'd had them in the Navy. They put as many men as they could get, usually about six, in the ring together blindfolded and the last one standing was the winner.

"No thanks," I said, "I don't want any of this."

"Well, look, don't worry. We'll only put one in from our club, then we won't be doing each other in. And I

204

know a stunt that used to be used in the Navy. Nobody up here will know it, and we're bound to win. As soon as the bell goes, drop on your hands and knees, crawl round until you feel a foot, then come straight up. They can't hit you when you're down there. Come straight up, keeping one hand on his body so you know exactly where he is, and let him have it before he knows what's happening. You can't lose that way."

And Joe Muggins thought, "That sounds feasible. I'll have a go." I think it was about five bob for the winner. Fantastic prize that, when you think we had to save up to get fourpence to go to the pictures.

Clang went the bell and away we all went. I dropped on to my hands, started feeling round. There it was, a foot. I put my glove on it. And the other foot came up and kicked me clean out of the ring. I didn't come round until the fight was over. So that finished my boxing career. I suppose I just didn't have the right instinct.

About the time I retired from the ring, an uncle of mine started dropping into the club. He was a little fat fellow, but in his younger days, about 1885 or so, he had been a professional runner. He had run in the Powderhall Sprints at Glasgow, one of several big professional meetings where athletes were paid to take part. He knew quite a bit about training and keeping fit and he started training me. He decided that I would make a runner, being as fit as I was and long and lean with it.

So I started running, jogging really, about 14 miles a night, from Hulme Church down through Chorlton, on to Stretford, down Derbyshire Lane to Eccles and then back. Then at weekends I was walking 30 to 40 miles. I got pretty fit, but although I won a silver medal in the half mile, it turned out I was a better walker than a runner. I won quite a few cups, including a big silver one in 1928 for a two-mile walk. I had a box full of medals too, but I gave them all away later, to different girls. Whatever girl I was with, I'd buy a little gold chain and give her the medal to hang round her neck. I lost them all that way.

I was not completely useless at running. The only snag was that the Amateur Athletic Association rules said you must join a club after a year of running unattached. I was friendly with Walter Ainsley of Salford Athletic Club, who was one of the top sprint merchants at the time, but the waiting list was too long for me to get in.

Eventually I joined the Hallamshire Harriers through meeting some of its members when I was camping in the Peak District near Castleton. They were all set up in running togs and when I asked could I join them they must have thought they could take the mickey, running me ragged for a couple of miles. But I kept speeding them up a bit and then a bit more and by the end of the run they'd had enough. I said, "Have we gone far enough? It doesn't feel as though we've done anything. Can we do another four or five miles and get some good out of it?" Then they realised they'd picked the wrong bloke.

So I joined their club. But it wasn't a very happy set-up. There were all sorts of petty jealousies. And what they euphemistically called pace-making was just gangsterism. A lot of the long distance events didn't have heats. They used to let everybody in, in a mass start, knowing that half would drop out before long. They weren't in to win, only to obstruct or kid the rest, so that their own club's front-runner could do well. Then when half the field had dropped out, exhausted from chasing stooges whose only purpose was to do exactly that, one of the blokes in it to win would signal that he was going to try a sprint. Then some of his mates would do their best to box in the opposition. It wasn't my idea of sport and eventually I gave it up.

I did get into another gym but it was a bit too rich for my blood. You had to pay to be in it. I joined because it was a school of arms. It was up near Oldham and what with the bus fares it was really more than I could afford. But I was in it for about six months, just long enough to enter their annual competitions. The bloke doing the tutoring had entered too and I thought that wasn't fair, but I kept quiet about the ex-naval bloke who had given us lessons in the Scouts, and managed to beat him in both single sticks and fencing.

Oh what a fuss! They couldn't figure it out. It was unheard of for a six-month student to beat the teacher! They asked me to resign and I did, but looking back on it, I think it was all a fiddle. I think the competition was just a money-making scheme with the teachers winning every time and putting up the same cups as prizes every year, to avoid having to buy new ones. It didn't work with me. I took away the cups I'd won, but they were soon covered in green mould because I couldn't be bothered with them. Anyway, they were only silver-plated. When the plating started to peel off, they were brass underneath.

So gradually my sporting days petered out. Everything was coming round to the modern way, highly organised, commercialised, encouraging back-biting, thuggery and jealousy. And in any case, it was getting in the way of my hiking and camping. I was always a lot better on my own. My tiny tent was reasonably weatherproof and I could pitch it beside a wall or an outcrop, even if I was on top of a mountain in a gale. There I would lie, warm and dry and snug, listening to the rain lashing down and the wind howling, watching the lightning.

And I'd be really happy. I'd think, I've beaten you, you sod! I've beaten you! I used to get this feeling that I'd beaten the mountain. I think climbers must have that same secret thought, once they get to the top. It's a tremendous feeling.

CHAPTER 25

TENTING TONIGHT

THERE were not many hikers and campers in 1924. A few odd scouts and walking clubs, that's all. The real craze did not start until after 1930, when there were special trains going out to Hayfield in Derbyshire.

Police used to question me in a friendly manner. "I've been up the field," said one. "Is that your tent up there?"

"Yes," I said.

"Well, you know you're going to have rheumatics and arthritis and everything else when you get older. The ground's full of water, it's damp all the time."

"I'm okay," I said, "I've got a rubber ground sheet."

"That's no good," he said. "It won't stop the cold and damp striking through. There's only one way to avoid it: nip into a field where there are some cows, move one from where it's lying and put your tent there. You'll find it's taken up all the moisture and warmed the ground too." He was deadly serious!

In another place, about three-quarters of a mile from a village, I'd got permission from a farmer to pitch my tent by a stream. Sunday morning, about 9am, I'd been up for a couple of hours and was just back from a run, when an old lady came across the field. "How long have you been here, lad?"

"I arrived last night," I said.

"When are you going home? Are you sure you're going home?" She was sure I had run away from home and she'd brought me a big breakfast of bacon and eggs and home-made bread. "Your mother will be worrying about you."

"She will if I don't get home tonight," I said. "She's used to this. I go out every weekend somewhere."

Eventually I convinced her and she then got interested in my home-made tent and blanket sleeping bag. Everybody was intrigued, in fact. Farmers couldn't figure out why anyone would want to sleep in a field on the wet grass with a bit of cloth over them. Where was the pleasure in it? Damned if I could tell 'em!

And sometimes of course it was anything but pleasure. You'd have a flood perhaps, or your tent blew away, although I soon learned how to avoid these problems. Then there were occasions when you couldn't avoid being in a field with cows, and cows are the most curious animals there are. As soon as you get inside your tent, they'll be all around it, just looking. And once they get used to it, one will come scratching her neck on the pole and eventually down comes the tent.

A pig is worse, though. Get one inside your tent and if it's a small one like mine, you just have to pick the tent up off it. It won't back out. It will stay there eating and when all the edible stuff has gone it will start on the leather straps of your rucksack. Horrible animal in a camp, is a pig.

Pleasure? I suppose it's something like a drug. It gets into your bloodstream. All I ever wanted to do was to be away, up in the mountains. My tent was always packed and ready, rolled up and hanging outside my pack. Everything else was there. All I had to do was put a bit of grub in the pack and I was off. I did it for years. I'd be doing it now, if I had feet fit to walk on. I'm happier in a tent than I am in a house.

A lot of odd things happened as I made my way up and down those hills. I met lots of people and some had quite an influence on my life. I got into all sorts of movements, into all sorts of places, amongst all kinds of people. I would never have had a chance to do this if I'd stayed home at weekends. As a matter of fact, the people I knew at home would never believe me when I told them who I had met and talked to. They don't believe me now, so what the hell!

I know it sounds sometimes as though it was one long holiday. Far from it! I never had enough money. When I was working, I used to get about a shilling spending money, because the family was struggling to keep going. My mother bought or made my clothes, but that shilling had to do for all my leisure time activities. A seat at the pictures, in the fourpenny's, was me finished for the weekend and a tuppenny bar of chocolate was an unthinkable extravagance.

So how could I afford to pay my fare into the hills? Well, first off, I'd head for Derbyshire, because that was the cheapest direction to take. It was fourpence on the tram to Hyde and fourpence to Stockport. Sometimes I would bring it down to threepence by walking part of the route. If I was heading out over the High Peak to Castleton, however, up over the moss on the top, I'd ride all the way to Stockport. This saved time, because when I was in work, knocking-off time was never earlier than noon on Saturday and I'd go straight from work, with just a boiler suit over my walking gear.

From Stockport I would then walk to Hayfield, where my weekend really began. I could usually be there round about teatime. Then in the long summer evenings, I could get away from Hayfield over the top, or over by Chinley

Churn or back towards Glossop, over William Clough. That was as good as a day's walk. Then, after tenting overnight, I had all day Sunday. But I could not afford to finish my walk in Glossop, Hayfield, Whaley or Chinley and pay my fare home from there. When the pleasure-walking was over, I had to start the trek to Stockport or Hyde, clutching my fourpence fare for the Sunday evening tram home.

Lots of people in those days would say, I don't know how you do it. I can't afford to go out camping every weekend. But they could have, if they'd done it like I did. Take utensils, for instance. A big camping firm supplied the well-off lads. I had one of their catalogues for years. A set of nesting pans (three saucepans and a frying pan with two clip-on handles) was about five shillings. But in Woolworth's nothing cost more than 6d, so you just bought three pans, which would fit inside each other. You bought three lids at tuppence each, so that came to eightpence, for each pan. Then you bought a frying pan for sixpence, and a couple of good solid clip-on handles at sixpence each.

You knocked out the rivets that held the original pan handles, then hammered the rivets back in to fill the holes so the pans wouldn't leak. And there was your perfectly good set of gear, for three shillings and sixpence instead of the five shillings that Camp and Sports Co-operators charged.

Then again, a tent like mine would have cost a good few quid. In fact it cost about three shillings, the price of the cloth at the mill where my mother worked. It was Egyptian cotton, very light and fine and ideal for tents. When it got wet, its fibres swelled and made it more rain proof. On top of that, I used to proof it myself. My pack was ex-Army – they cost two shillings new or half that reconditioned and were very tough. Mine lasted for years. It was still in good condition when I gave it away.

So for a few shillings you could go camping. It meant walking, but 20 or 30 miles a day meant nothing to me. Even when I was only eight or nine, I would go out over Pendle after school. Four o'clock I'd go out and I'd be on top of Pendle by quarter to five. It's quite a climb up the Big End as they call it, the Nelson end, but I would be up to the top and down again by six, in time for tea. About eight miles, including going up and down Pendle. I suppose it conditioned me from an early age, so it was natural that I should be a good walker.

By about 1934 I was in several clubs and organisations. The Peveril Club, the Bogtrotters, all tough walkers. It was the popular thing to wear badges and I had a lapel full. There were scores of clubs. The Ramblers Federation for instance. I helped to get that going with Tom Stephenson and old Jimmy Ambler – Ambler the Rambler. I was knocking about with his daughter for a long time, till she found somebody with more money and better looking!

I met lots of people, many of them when access to mountains was the big thing. Gamekeepers used to chase us off the mountains, but eventually they marked out one or two paths and we kept to them. But then they started setting up barriers across the paths, and the Ramblers Federation held the first of what was to become an annual event – a big protest rally at Winnats Pass in Derbyshire.

That was where I met a famous playwright of the day, L du Garde Peach, a queer name. I think he had acted in films and he eventually set up the Peak Theatre at Hope, converted from a big barn. Anyway, he was at the rally. I met him, but I didn't bother with him. I didn't like him, or the way he was going on. He was just publicity-seeking. It was the same with his theatre. He put on about two shows a year, at summer and Christmas. They became a cult. If you were local you couldn't get in, the audience was made up of important Londoners.

The Ramblers Federation was also taken over. Nine-tenths of the members were from the North, but the London boys came up and took it over, renamed it the Ramblers Association and set up a new scale of salaried officials. Another example of commercialisation.

Then I was in at the start of the Youth Hostels Association. I had teamed up with a Manchester bloke, hike-camping together at weekends and his sister asked us to help set up a scheme to find places for walkers to rest and shelter in. "We don't need it," we said. "We've got tents."

"Well," she said, "there's a lot who haven't. Come and give us a lift."

And she held out the usual inducements: Tilly Flop and Aggie Hasnowt would be there, she said. So on the strength of them providing some wenches for us, we went down to Maeshafn, a little place just outside Mold.

And that was the beginning of the YHA. It was a damn good thing in its early years. It was cheap – a shilling a night, plus threepence to hire a thin cotton sleeping bag if you didn't have your own. You got blankets and a bed and the sleeping bag saved them providing sheets and kept the blankets cleaner. You could cook your own meals or buy them. Tea was a shilling, breakfast the same and a packed lunch of two or three sandwiches, an apple and an orange, was sixpence.

So, for three shillings and sixpence a day, which was

pretty reasonable, you got more or less full board. The only rule they had to make in the early days was that you were allowed only three nights in any hostel and then you had to move on to make room for others.

Eventually I was made a committee member. We met in a building in Queen Street, Manchester, which was used by various social services and charities. Practically all the work in the hostels was done by voluntary working parties and it was my job to set these up: bricklayers, sanitary engineers, plumbers, joiners and lots of unskilled labourers, blokes to push barrows around and dig trenches, girls to cook rough-and-ready meals. No-one paid hostel fees, but they all paid for the food or brought their own. They must have saved the Association thousands of pounds, transforming derelict places, getting water to them, even digging wells.

All this, the committee work etc, brought me into contact with many people outside my humble sphere. But it never seemed to alter my speech. Me and my little rebel mind; I was still proud of my Lancashire burr when others were feverishly trying to get rid of theirs.

And it was amazing the things I got pushed into doing! I think it was just because I had a knack of saying things slightly differently, not in accent but in content. I didn't know a thing about most of the jobs I got landed with. It didn't impress me. If anything, it irritated me. I was Joe Muggins again. It was always: "Come on, Paul, you can do it ... you're the best at this."

So I got lumbered with all the donkey work and all the trouble, even if it was only arguing with a farmer about going across his field. It took a long, long time for it to seep in, that I should have been at the back, shouting somebody else's name: "Go on, you do it!"

CHAPTER 26

MAD LEM WRAGGE

SOME of my oddest experiences were not while wander-camping, but at a fixed camp, in a field at Nab Farm, below Whiteley Nab, Glossop. The farmer, originally from Bakewell, was Lemuel Wragge. What a name, and what a character! He talked sensibly enough, but he'd do anything, whether it conformed to the acceptable norms of behaviour or not. As you will see.

We were quite happy, Bump Barnsley, Babs Cooper, Smitty and me, with our big ex-Army bell tent, in which we could safely leave bits of kit all week. Old Lem was charging us about ninepence a week each, for which we could also use certain farm facilities. But by the start of the next season there were a lot more tents; and one bunch of newcomers, bright sparks all of them, obviously looked on the rest of us as scum.

There were four of them, test drivers for the old Leyland lorry builders, or it might have been Foden's. They were pretty well-off because of a wangle they'd worked out. Instead of putting scrap iron in the ballast box when they drove a test chassis out of the factory, they were loading up with motor parts and selling them. Not only dishonest, but arrogant too, but they got their comeuppance when they tried to take over Lem Wragge's farmhouse.

He had thrown open one or two rooms for people to stay in the farm at weekends and the farm had become like a clubhouse. These bright lads were bringing their girls and mates from town and when they got into the farmhouse, nobody else had a look in. I was in the barn with Lem when his wife came out from the farm. "Can you move them?" she said. "I can't get near the fire." We went in. On the ground floor there was only one living room, plus a kitchen and dairy and they had completely commandeered the living room, sitting four deep around the fire. Nobody could get near. Lem tried to be reasonable, but they just jeered at him.

He came out fuming but didn't say anything. He firmly tied up the doors, front and back, then went round the back to the well, dipped a big sack in it, climbed up on the roof and put the wet sack over the chimney pot. The windows were tiny and only one would open. It took us nearly a week to clean the room and the smell lingered for weeks. But that arrogant lot didn't try it again.

Another time, some other hikers tried the same thing. Once they'd got their pots of tea, they crowded inside with them and when old Lem tried to get into his own living room, they just told him to go away, using a four-letter euphemism. Now at this time Lem had a very savage goose, a real monster that had to be tied up when people wanted to cross the farmyard. And as these ignorant louts carried on inside, having a rare old party with their girls and their pots of tea and packed lunches, Lem once again tied up the farmhouse doors. Then he pushed the goose in through the little window and pulled it shut.

Whew! If ever the horror people made a film of it, it would be a best seller. It would pack the cinemas, the scene that went on in there. That goose was not only vicious, it was frightened, too. It was flapping and honking and snapping at people. What a sight! The women were screaming and fainting, while the blokes were yelling and fighting each other to get out. They all did, eventually, but they never came back.

Mad as a hatter was Old Lem Wragge. Another bunch of lads staying in a bungalow near the farmhouse were getting drunk and keeping everyone awake with wild parties late every night. They refused to leave, so Lem came to me one day and said, "I'm going to try an experiment. Will you help me?"

Knowing his tendencies, I should have refused, but out of curiosity I went back to the farmhouse with him. He was making gunpowder! He had mixed all his ingredients and someone had told him it was more powerful if it was granulated. You did this by soaking it, drying it slowly in a pan and when you had a big cake of the stuff, you granulated it by pounding it with a hammer!

Anyway, the drying process was too slow for old Lem and after a week or so he decided to speed it up. He lit a Primus stove, put a thick slab of walling stone on it and sat the pan on top of that. It was a big pan. There must have been about six pounds of the damp mixture in it. "Come on," he said. "You've just to keep stirring till it begins to cake. Just don't let it settle."

"Oh, no!" I said. "I want nowt to do with this." And I left him to it. A bit later, I was in the lane outside the farm and could see him through the window. And just at that moment he managed to get a spark into his mix. It was like a giant welding torch. A white-hot flame shot straight up, a foot across and five feet high, like the tail-end of a moon rocket. It went on for three or four minutes, with Lem dancing around trying to throw sacks over it. It burned straight through them, set fire to the window frame, the door, and some furniture. We put it out finally with buckets of water, but it was a right mess.

It didn't cure Lem, though. Next thing to annoy him was when some bright little campers started washing with soap in a trough fed from a spring which flowed onwards to another farm. Lem played hell with them for polluting the other farm's cattle-water, but they just laughed at him. "Well," he said, "I'll stop the next 'un." So I'm standing at the farm door, watching these lads coming up for a wash. "This should be interesting, I thought. Let's see how he handles *this*!"

They'd got their soap out and had just stripped down to the waist, when I felt a weight on my shoulder. I looked round to find a full 12-bore shotgun resting on my shoulder, a good two feet of it pointing out in front of me. And before I could duck or even shout, bang! bang! He'd let fly with both barrels. He aimed to one side of them, but some were still cut by chips of stone flying off the wall. And me? Well, I was deaf for a month. When I played hell with him for using me as a rest for his shotgun, he said, by way of explanation, "I hadn't time to move you. I had to catch 'em."

I found out later why he'd put up with us campers on his land: he had no money, no stock to speak of and a deep aversion to work. I also heard that he was in and out of prison for fiddling and thieving. Not a big surprise, I suppose. Mad as a hatter, he was.

CHAPTER 27

LEFT-WINGING

THE camping business was mainly a weekend job. During the week I'd become involved in a left-wing club, Hyndman Hall, in Liverpool Street, Salford, which I mentioned earlier. The ground floor was a social club, with billiard table and bar and the first floor was a dance hall, open every night, with tuition and records to dance to. It only cost a copper or two, so it was quite popular with poorer teenagers. And on the top floor was a gymnasium with a full-size boxing ring.

I showed the trainers how to swing clubs and did a bit of running practice with them. But their limit was around the block, so I dropped that and once again tried to learn a bit of boxing. I had two practices with them and twice I got my clock knocked round. I decided they were just using me as a punch bag and not trying to teach me anything, so I stuck to the social club.

I had long discussions with two chaps down there. One was Walter Greenwood, who lived in Hankinson Street and later became quite famous. The other was an odd bod called Frank Spencer, who taught himself Russian by painfully translating novels in Russian which he got from the library, using a second-hand dictionary he'd found on a Shudehill market stall. In the early 30s he went to Russia and ended up teaching English at a holiday resort on the Black Sea. I lost touch with him when the war started.

Greenwood and Spencer were both intellectuals. I

wasn't. I hadn't the time in those days, though I certainly agreed with left-wing theory and had lived a sort of left-wing life. You do when you're down at the bottom. But knowing the life I had led, the bad jobs and the time on the road, they couldn't understand how I couldn't see the whole picture. I'd read very few of the so-called 'essential' books. I could understand what they were on about, but I used to get bored with them. Greenwood and Spencer could not understand why I didn't know as much as they did. I spent hours trying to persuade them that when you're physically involved in this sort of thing, you only see your immediate circle.

I thought then and I still think now, that the intellectuals who see the whole picture have usually only read about it. They are the ones who stand at the back reading the books, while the poor slobs like me are at the front, getting their brains kicked in. It applies to everything, from work to war: the blokes who do the job usually know the least about it.

I had mentioned during one of our many discussions that I had been to see one or two left-wing plays by the Theatre of Action, and Greenwood obviously remembered, because one night he told me he had written a one-act play. Would I show it to them and see what they thought? He brought it for us to look at and Frank, being a literary sort of bloke, said: "Get a bit of string and hang the bloody lot in the bog-house. That's all it's good for."

I was a bit more circumspect. I argued that the Theatre of Action couldn't possibly stage it, because the characters didn't ring true, for a start. They were ordinary people out of work and he'd got them talking meaningless, wishy-washy dialogue, with tennis club accents. The sort of thing you hear in Sunday school pantomimes. It was terrible.

It was a weak story anyway, involving a bloke falling down and banging his head on a counter and whilst unconscious having a dream about a labour exchange in which the clerks address everybody as 'Sir' and give them cups of tea and the dole is enough to live on.

It could have been a good satire at that time, but not the way he did it. He was getting his characters talking before they made an entrance. Couldn't get his characters on, couldn't get them off. Everything was wrong. He had a cast of about 40 and only about seven or eight speaking parts. He wanted a complete labour exchange building with big desks, filing cabinets and cupboards and long queues of people, reaching off stage.

When the Theatre of Action went barn-storming with their agitprop verse-readings and one-act plays, it might be in a little Labour Party room with an audience of only about 40 or so. The stage would be a sort of raised platform one foot high and ten feet square, and Greenwood wanted them to stage all this lot on it! Even so, he conned me into taking it home and typing it up for him. He also asked me to straighten it out a bit, but I couldn't make sense of it. I would have had to have rewritten it completely and I didn't think I was capable of writing a play. And of course, when I showed it to the Theatre of Action, they just laughed.

I gave it back to him, softening the blow as much as I could and he announced: "I've started writing a full-length play!" Eventually he brought in a dozen pages of what eventually became *Love On The Dole*. It was worse than the one-act play! Frank just gave up. "Have a pint, and call it a draw," he said.

I read it. It was hopelessly written. He was doing little

character sketches of the people he knew in Hankey Park, Salford, which was very laudable, but he didn't have them talking as though they came from the poor areas of Salford, the back end of Ellor Street. I said, "I've had enough with the other. I don't want to be bothered with this." He got the hump at this, came in the odd time or two, but eventually disappeared.

But 18 months later, what should we see at the Salford Hippodrome, at the top end of Cross Lane, but *Love on the Dole*. There was a Councillor Crabtree in it, playing the part of a workhouse master. In real life he was actually the master at Salford workhouse, which was a real hell hole; and here he was performing in this play.

Well, I had to see it and it wasn't bad. But it was billed BY WALTER GREENWOOD AND RONALD GOW. Gow was a schoolmaster in Altrincham and he had obviously managed to re-write the dialogue and stage the thing properly. It went around the northern theatres and was quite popular. I think it was the Fortescue Players, a repertory group from Rusholme, who toured the North with it and started to make money for Greenwood. Eventually it got to the West End. It was revolutionary, a kitchen sink drama as they were later called. They'd never seen anything like it and it took off.

Finally it became a film and made Greenwood a heap of money. I never saw Greenwood again and neither did the girl from the next street who had subsidised him, buying him clothes and fags when he was out of work. He married an actress and took off to Capri. The last I heard of him was a couple of letters only a few years back, just before he died. He wanted some Salford children's songs for a musical he was doing. He was in the Isle of Man then, tax evading.

CHAPTER 28

CURTAIN CALLS

WHEN I became more involved with the Theatre of Action, once again I ran into the thinking people. It was no ordinary dramatic society. It was infested with left-wing theatrical intellectuals. They weren't interested in going on stage and acting a part, no matter how left-wing the production. They were reading Stanislavski and wanted to do it all Russian-style.

But people just weren't ready for it. We'd go into a Labour Party club full of ordinary people, who were familiar with all the musical comedies and popular films. When our lot started putting on very complicated and abstruse pieces of agitprop verse, they were lost, because they didn't know what it was all about. And I sympathised with them, though I only had myself to blame, having got myself into it as a non-acting member.

The leading spirits in this were Joan Littlewood and Jimmy Miller, who later changed his name and became the folk-singer Ewan McColl. Littlewood was the worst of the lot, insisting that everybody should learn to act. I had a lot of work to do, particularly when a production was coming up. Three or four of us made the scenery and props, but twice a week, on acting school night, she would stop us and insist that we go into the classroom. The first time she collared me, she said, "Come on, everybody's got to learn, in case they're needed." I went down with her.

"Stand at the door," she said, "and shut yourself out.

Now, you're coming into a cafe. You stand by the door and look round for the person you've come to meet. Then you go over to him, say hello and sit down. Let's see how you do it." I did it to the best of my ability, which was about nil, and when I'd done, she called me every name she could lay tongue to. So I said, "Whoa! Wait a minute. It's no good telling me I'm no good at it. I know I'm no good at it. I've never had any teaching, I have no intention of going on a stage under any circumstances and if you don't like it, you can go up there and paint your own bloody scenery."

I believe they had a committee meeting about it, where I was described as being subversive, anti-left, or whatever name they had for it then. But they couldn't get enough people to help out and I was one of the Joe Mugginses that used to push their bloody handcart through the streets. So I stayed on, but we never got to be kissing cousins.

Our rehearsal and meeting rooms were in Grosvenor Street, All Saints, and later in two rooms over a shop in Stretford Road. Miller and Littlewood were not very popular and I don't know whether they decided to leave or were invited to leave, but they packed up and went to London and started something called the Miller Theatre. One of my mates, Sid Deitch, a Jewish lad from Cheetham Hill, was a good actor and they persuaded him to join them there. He wrote me one or two optimistic letters and then we lost touch.

The next I heard of Miller and Littlewood was just before the war. They'd got hold of an old building near Kendal and started a group called Theatre Workshop. It moved back to London eventually and became quite famous. Several West End hits came out of it.

Meanwhile, a chap named Harold Olsberg took over as our director and the plays improved. They became working class plays which people could understand, instead of exercises in abstruse stagecraft. But it was still classed as left-wing and agitprop, and none of it was licensed by the Lord Chamberlain. So, apart from the barnstorming, we had to create a private theatre. Membership was £1 a year, or it could have been only ten shillings. For that you were admitted to the four full-length plays which we put on each year, on the top floor of the old Athenaeum Club, at the back of Mosley Street. It had a good theatre, fully professional, with a big stage, drawn curtains, flats for scenery, side and back curtains, lights that dimmed, plus spots and floods. The only difference was that it had ordinary foldaway chairs, so that they could clear the room and use it for dancing.

Our barnstorming material could only be shown where there was a private membership, like a Labour Club, or a CP or YCL meeting. There was certainly nothing pretty-pretty about it – no Desert Songs for us. Our oppos in Liverpool were pinched for putting on an American play, *Waiting for Lefty*. I believe someone was fined over it.

Once again though, and despite the best efforts of Harold Olsberg, the real aims of our group began to get lost. I think with it being full of intellectuals, they'd lost sight of the actuality. We had only one or two working lads. The rest were teachers, white collar office types, shopkeepers and a couple of girls who didn't work at all and lived in Prestwich, right outside the working class sphere, playing at being working class. It was a cult, and I used to get sick of it all. I'd see blokes who hadn't a clue about accents, trying to talk like ordinary working men.

226

But they had educated voices and just couldn't do it. Not only that, they couldn't even act like ordinary working people.

It worried me, but I learned to live with it. Anyway, it never impressed me as doing any good. I used to say to people, "You're wasting your time." Our audiences, being left-wing, were already converted. "Well," my colleagues would say, "they need educating." I remember saying on one occasion: "Let's prove this point. Let's ask some of the people after it's over. Let's go down amongst them and ask them what it was all about." And I'm prepared to swear that not one in 50 of them got it right! And our messages were by no means subtle.

But everybody had a good time and they all thought they were doing a great thing for the cause and I seemed to be the only one who sort of sat outside, worrying about it. But as I say, I learned to live with it. I even had a good time, once I'd forgotten they were doing everything wrong.

Sometimes we put on public plays, which, while not exactly being licensed, didn't offend the eyes and ears of the watch committee. One was a peace play called *Miracle at Verdun*. This was when Joan Littlewood was still with us. It was staged at the Manchester Free Trade Hall and ran for a week. The basic story was that an angel comes down to a mass grave, where all the First World War soldiers are buried together, and German, French and English all return to life and troop out. All these former corpses set out to walk home, but most of their wives have new husbands, there's no work for them and not enough food. And the governments are worried, knowing they are going to start asking questions about the way the war was run.

There were about 24 scenes and each 15-second change was done in a blackout; from a lonely crossroads in Germany to the French Prime Minister's bedroom and from that to the Cenotaph in London. We had quite a bit of fun, making people up. I was actually on stage this time, as a soldier who had been shot almost to pieces.

The last scene was the League of Nations, with about 40 people on stage, deciding to combine their armies, to wipe out the marching dead. It was a good story and message, and on the opening night, before we started, a famous Lord Mayor of Manchester, Alderman Joe Toole, got up on stage, and made a really good peace speech – there should be no more war, and all the usual things that these people spout. What the audience didn't know, and what we didn't know until a day or two later, was that the following night he was in Lancaster, making a recruiting speech to try and get people to join the army. Such is politics.

Of course we had the usual set of calamities. The French Prime Minister's bedroom scene, for instance, had to have a very expensive looking bed. We tied a rope round four orange boxes, put a pole at the back and made a canopy over it, all in fancy materials which people had brought from home, plus a fancy bedspread. With a white spot on it and dim-lit curtains all around, it was very effective – except on the first night when the Lord Mayor was there. Littlewood, too eager again, hadn't left us enough time to set up the scene and someone failed to tie the boxes together tightly enough. Just as the lights came up on the Prime Minister and his woman getting into bed, the rope came undone and the pair of them disappeared into the middle of the orange boxes. To us it was a catastrophe of the first water, but it certainly amused the audience.

Barnstorming was even more basic. We had to push stuff about on handcarts. Another bloke and I did it, mainly because we were out of work. I've pushed handcarts as far as Stalybridge and pushed them back again on a Sunday morning. I often wonder if the nice young men in the Altrincham Garrick and Swinton Operatic Society would do the same.

CHAPTER 29

BACK TO REALITY

Paul's bedsit, Carlton Road, Whalley Range.

A WHILE after this, I left the Hyndman Hall club, more or less under a cloud, through no fault of my own.

I was camping near New Mills and one of a party of YCL [*Young Communists' League*] hikers recognised me as being in the anti-blackshirt squad. The hikers' leader asked if I could help set up a children's summer camp in a farmer's field. Permission was quite easy as I knew the farmer fairly well.

The hikers' leader then said that various left-wing organisations had already promised to raise money for the camp. Could I get Hyndman Hall to help? Back in Salford, I put it to the committee. They agreed and started running raffles in the club. One night a week the dance hall takings went towards it and some of the boxers put on monthly bouts in aid of the fund. We must have raised £200 or £300, a hell of a lot of money in those days. Others must have been producing similar amounts.

The following year, the farmer asked when the children's camp was going to be set up, so I went to inquire at the YCL room in Cheetham Hill. The bloke had disappeared and so had the money. Then the Hyndman Hall committee started looking a bit sideways at me and I felt the strain of it, so I retired, not very gracefully, but I got out. A couple of years later I found that I shouldn't have felt so guilty. Since it closed, the club has seen various uses. A few years ago it was a garment factory. But from what I heard, it was a very lucrative business even when it was a club.

I was beginning to lose faith in the organised left-wing. Everywhere I turned, I found phoneys, self-seekers; and very often there was no way to kick the feet from under them. The only way was not to let yourself get used. I got out of it.

There was another reason for my leaving Hyndman Hall. Once again it boiled down to the difference between doers and thinkers. For about three years, I had been helping three old ladies. One was crippled with arthritis and her husband was bedfast. I used to do her shopping for her; washing as well, and a bit of housework. The other two lived nearby and one had a wheelchair. She let me borrow it and I would take them all out, in turn, so they could choose their own things at the shops. Or I'd take them out for an hour in the park when the weather was fine and the birds were singing.

I had been talking to some of the younger end at the Hyndman Club, suggesting we could expand what I was doing, maybe do odd jobs for people. But when the committee, the book readers and the theorists and the thinkers, got to know about it, they kiboshed it straight away. "Oh no," they said. "If you help people who need help, you are only assisting the Capitalist Government."

Well, I could never in a thousand years be brought around to this way of thinking. I could see the point they were trying to make, but I couldn't believe in it. To see somebody going short, to see somebody in real trouble and then condemn anybody that helped them because it was going to assist the Government! No, I couldn't have this. And by the time I'd finished saying so, in the necessary basic English, I was even more of a *persona non grata*. So I moved out.

I kept on with the helping scheme while I could. When I was out of work I'd go round during the day and when I was working I'd go in the evening. The shops were open until 8pm then. And I tried, with some success, to expand it. I was still fairly involved with the YHA, as an appointer of wardens and I was still leading the work teams, furnishing new hostels and repairing old ones. We had plumbers, painters and decorators, builders, electricians – a lot of people who willingly gave up their weekends. I talked to some of them and one or two were interested. One bloke started a scheme in

232

Sheffield, just him and a few pals, giving up an hour or two each week to help old people.

In Manchester, I got three or four people doing a bit; anything we could do without money. We unblocked sinks, reslated roofs and rebuilt backyard walls that kids had knocked down. We cleaned carpets too and generally did a lot of donkey work for people who were incapable of doing it.

It came to an end after about four years, but I never regretted leaving the club. Their idea of helping people was to go around giving lectures on dialectical materialism and the life of Lenin. That doesn't help an old lady who can't get out. It doesn't buy her groceries.

That's my view, anyway. But then, I'm only one bloke.

REMEMBERING

MIKE HARDING, *Manchester folk singer and comedian, recalls his days with Paul.*

"I met Paul Graney in the mid-60s. It was at the Old House At Home in Lower Blackley, Manchester, where I ran a folk club in what must be one of the strangest positions of any pub in England. Surrounded by the steam pipes and cables of the ICI dye factory, the inn was on an island of land, coveted but never acquired by the huge multi-national.

That Sunday night, Paul was dressed as he always dressed, summer and winter: belted brown raincoat, sandals with socks on, beret on his head and ubiquitous fuming pipe clenched in his crooked teeth.

He was to become a friend, adviser and companion on collecting forays into the pubs of Lancashire and Cheshire and gave me and many other young singers song after song, copied out in his thin, neat handwriting. He was probably the most important source of the tradition for many of us, during those early days of the folk revival. Many of the songs I sang during my apprenticeship had been collected or collated by Paul, often on one of his battered old tape recorders.

He was terrible at indexing and cataloguing, but always seemed to know where everything was in his chaos of a room and could lay his hands on a ballad or a tune in minutes: "Aye, I got a version of that in the forties. I gave it to Bert Lloyd."

He was a witty man and the fire of laughter was hardly ever out of his eyes. He made a good friend, but never forgave a wrong. He suffered fools not at all and if he suspected anyone of humbug or conceit, he'd bring them crashing down with the dry wit of his Lancashire mill town tongue, leaving the victim knowing he'd been dropped on, but not quite knowing how. I remember he took a particular dislike to one revival singer and delighted in taking the mickey out of him. It was sometimes painful to watch.

Paul's politics were of the left. He supported the underdog and the oppressed and had that wonderful dissenter's distrust of all authority. 'No man is good enough to be another man's master' might well have been his motto, for he certainly lived as though it were. And his belief in the basic nobility of the working class led him to see the last flowers of folk music and song that he was collecting as the dying gasps of a tradition and culture that had either been destroyed or hijacked.

He distrusted intellectuals too, unless they also had some hands-on experience, and he kept his most cutting scorn for what he called the 'method' singers, the actor-trained school that he felt was moulding a stable of mannered and artificial singers.

Pictures have been flashing across my mind as I have been writing this: Paul with a pint and his pipe in Bacup on Nutters' Day ... the pair of us in the crammed back room of a pub watching the Antrobus Soul Cakers ... the beach at Whitby during the resort's famous folk festival, Paul in his raincoat in the blazing sun, finally stripping down to his cardigan as he and Tom Gilfellon (of the Northumberland folk group the High Level Ranters) tore each other to rags of laughter.

Paul was a proud man: proud of his roots, proud of the hills and the people he came from, and totally free of deceit or malice. He was a great collector and a great friend. I am proud and glad that he was part of mine and my family's life."

OTHER TRIBUTES

MARIE LITTLE *folk singer, West Rainton, near Durham.*
"Paul enriched my life, not only through the folk material he gathered, but with wonderful anecdotes and stories and nice touches like gifts of sweets he had made. I feel honoured and privileged to have been one of his close friends. He was so different from anyone I had met. He was non-conformist, intelligent, analytical, amazingly interesting and working class through and through. He made a tremendous impact on my life and will always hold a prominent place in both my memory and my heart."

BILL LEADER *former record producer and senior lecturer in recording studies, University College, Salford.*
"I met Paul Graney only once. It was at Southport on a 12th of July. I was there to record the wide variety of marching bands in the Orange Day parade. Paul was there because the event existed. I'd heard tales of his insatiable curiosity about customs and their practice; of how he was amongst the pioneers of the use of domestic tape recorders to document traditions. We sat for an hour or so, talking as two people do who know of each other but have never met. Now, many years on, what sticks in my mind is the rich flow of information, speculation and theorising that came from him. Each topic and idea had his own personal curl on it, giving things a different perspective from the one I had. I remember thinking at the time, this man lives in the same world as me, but his eyesight's better."

RHODA ADAMSON *Sale, Cheshire.*

"Our paths crossed when I was working for the Education Service at the North West Museum of Science and Industry, which was then in Grosvenor Street, All Saints, Manchester. Paul often came in, especially on days when textile machinery was working. One day he asked if I knew about the stick loom made by the American plains Indians to make mats for summer shelters, because visiting children might like to know how it worked. A couple of weeks later, he brought in something in a plastic bag – a working model, made with carefully selected sticks from the garden outside his flat. Grass for weaving had been more of a problem, so he had made a trip to the banks of the Mersey, to find the right length and thickness of dried grasses."

PAT RYAN *folk singer, Blackrod, Bolton, Lancashire.*

"I used to sing at a lot of folk clubs in the Manchester area in the 1970s and Paul Graney seemed to be at all of them. He was usually in the corner, with his pipe and tape recorder, always ready to talk. As he was a man who didn't suffer fools gladly, I was happy to be considered one of his friends."

BERNARD WRIGLEY *actor and singer, Horwich, Bolton, Lancashire.*

"Paul loved going to the local clubs. Local was anywhere within the bus route – he missed the final part of many an evening because the last bus (as always) left at an inconvenient time. I've still got the typewritten sheets he gave me, songs like 'The Highwayman of Blackstone Edge' and 'Our English Country Garden'. I imagine him, still with his baccy, collecting songs in that great folk club in the sky."

GRAHAM BREEDS *retired teacher.*

"I met Paul when I was head of education services at the North West Museum of Science and Industry in Manchester. I soon found him to be Graney by name and grainy by nature – a forthright and honest man, who never minced his words. He had lived a life on the edge for so many years that he cared very little for material things, except insofar as they affected his long obsession with the music and the folklore of his beloved Lancashire. I remember him with respect and admiration."

LESLEY BOARDMAN *widow of folksinger Harry Boardman, Gatley, Stockport.*

"Paul was best known to Harry and me for the wealth of dialect material≠– songs, poems, tacklers' tales, recipes – which came through our letterbox, all impeccably typed by Paul himself. It never ceased to amaze us that this bluff, elderly working man, had immersed himself so completely in the folk culture of the area and was so generous in his dissemination of material to those who appreciated it.

Paul's attempts to foster the image of a somewhat crusty old bachelor hid a softer side to his personality – his great love of children and his ability to enter into their world. Our sons, Tim and Robin, well remember Paul inspiring many of their childhood adventures, especially trips into Derbyshire to explore the caves and to hunt for fossils and specimens of Blue John stone – equipped, of course, with ropes and hammers.

Perhaps the highlight of their year, though, was Bonfire Night, when Paul would orchestrate the whole evening (much to my relief). He always knew where to put the pinwheels, the best positions for the Roman candles and he provided the tastiest treacle toffee of all time. Best of all was his positive enjoyment of the proceedings and his ability to turn the event into a few hours of magic. It was a privilege to share our lives with such a man."

THEY TALKED TO PAUL

A lad who carried his father's fighting clogs; another recalling boyhood scrapes; women remembering life in the workhouse, or working at the pit-head; old poacher; young tramp – the depth and range of Paul's curiosity can be seen in the following edited interviews. Paul believed that ordinary people such as these were the strongest threads in the cloth of history.

Purring ... a harmless-sounding word that hides a vicious reality. Purring was clog fighting and men used their skill at this brutal sport to fight for much-needed money. **Billy Findlow** had no option but to be there ... he carried his father's fighting clogs.

"The men was all colliers, forge men, all in rough, heavy jobs and this was one of their sports or pastimes. Two men used to stand face to face, hands on each other's shoulders. If you let go, you lost.

You'd to keep kickin' as fast and hard as you could and the first on the floor, the first to let go, or the first to give over, lost. They could be kickin' for a few bob or a few pound.

They had their own special clogs, fancy leather, highly polished. I used to carry my father's, wrapped in a white silk muffler. I think the clogs was better dressed than me! They were red, fancy cut, brass nails. The toe cap was a big brass plate.

They had to be polished underneath, inside, outside, all the nails, the lot. When you had a good pair of kicking clogs, you was halfway to winning your match.

They mostly used to make the match in the beer house. Over a few gills, they'd say, "I've got a good kicker here." And they'd get the match on, one boozer against the other. More often than not, the landlord would put the money up, £5 a match, £10 … Then the lads would have a whip-round and put their money on.

There were no prizes, not for the actual match. If the landlord won a fiver, you might get £1 off him.

They'd have a referee, generally a big rough bloke. He held his cap up in his hand and when he brought it down, that was your sign. You got kicking as fast and hard as you could. You could kick as often as you wanted, but when you went down on the deck, that was it, you was finished.

You mustn't let go! I've seen them rip a shirt arm off, but they've still got hold with the other hand. I've seen them holdin' the flesh.

My old man was pretty good at it. He used to climb up them in some way. He used to leave the floor with his feet and that was it until somebody dropped, either him or the other fellow. He was a local champion.

But you wondered how they kept going at it. Their legs! Some were like corrugated tin where they'd been kicked. They talk about these hard cases. I wonder if these young 'uns would have a go at it. I've often thought I'd like to, but I think it's a little bit too rough. Funny though, I've seen a lot of matches and a lot of blood, but I've only ever seen one leg broken.

My old feller once had a match with a bloke called Johnson who was six foot. I think there was some bad blood … It was got up for a Sunday, on the Dingle. That was a piece of ground where they used to tip slurry and dirt from Bradford pit, at the back of Philip's Park, right where the old United football ground used to be. It used to start on Bank Street and go over to Clayton Vale. There was big hollows and they used to get in these hollows for

242

the kicking matches.

This day with Johnson, they was kicking away and suddenly down they go, but they didn't stop kicking and then my old man's back on his feet and still kicking, but he didn't kick on t' legs. He kicked old Johnson's ribs in! I think he had three or four ribs broke. It was an Ancoats Hospital job.

My old man was champion of his boozer for years and years. Only five foot and about nine and a half stone at the very most. He retired undefeated champion. That's not swanking, it's true.

One time there was an argument with a boozer across the road. This bloke was champion of the New Inn and my old man had been the Cricketer's Rest champ. They argued that this feller was better than my old feller had ever been. And he decided to come out of retirement and kick this one.

That match was the first time I ever got a ten shilling note given me. Old Preston at the boozer give it me. Anyway, there it was, this match, on the Dingle. On they goes and away he kicks. The old feller won. How much I don't know, but that's when Preston give me the ten bob, so he must have had a few quid from it.

His clogs were the pride of the house. You daren't touch them, they was wrapped in that silk and after a match they was washed. Soap and water, then dried and given a polish till you could see your face in them.

You cleaned the irons too, picked all the bits out of them. They had strappings between the irons, a bit of leather belting. Kicking was winter and summer and the strapping was to stop their feet slipping on the hard ground. Mind you, I don't think their feet ever touched the ground once they'd come up!

Where I lived there was two works. There was Bradford pit and there was Johnson's wire works, but it was always known as Johnson's forge. At Johnson's, whatever job you was doing, you was a forge man. It's still called the Forge. There's a boozer called the Forge, which must have got its name for that reason.

They employed a good few hundred men and you was either down the pit or at the forge, one of those two. And if you wasn't working at one of those two and you wasn't travelling out of town, you was on the dole.

Earlier, Billy talked of destitute families, unable to pay the rent and put out on the street by the bailiffs, or worse ...

Another thing was the Board of Guardians if you was really hard up. You'd get a visitor. He'd come round and walk in the house and he'd say, you can sell this, you can sell that. And if you'd no money and you couldn't eat cos you'd nowt to sell, nowt to pawn, they'd give you a food ticket. They used to allow an adult three shillings and a penny for a week's living. A child under 14 was one shilling and tuppence.

If you couldn't manage on that, and you'd been thrown out, there was only one place for you and that was the workhouse. Dreadful place."

MRS ANDERTON, *an 80-year-old from Salford, could have vouched for that. She had been in the workhouse as a young and pregnant girl.*

"I always remember 1922, when I was desperate. I had to go into the workhouse. Them days were bad ... terrible. I had to be up at six of a morning. Have my breakfast. Be on duty at eight stoning the corridors. Miles and miles round. I'd finish at four o'clock and we'd all have to be in bed for six."

I'd do that from Monday to Friday. Weekends we had to ourselves to go to church and that, but I'd never seen outside the door until a fortnight before my baby was born and Dr Giles got me into Hope Hospital.

They was very hard days for anybody in the workhouse. I was in that long, I made a poetry up:

The workhouse is long from end to end.
When I came in I found no friend.
I left my home with an aching heart,
And found no one to take my part.
Every night when the moon shines bright,
In the workhouse I make my bed.
Not to sleep, but to sob and to weep,
And many a bitter tear I shed.
Although I'm in the workhouse now,
And sad it is my lot,
I try to bear with a contented heart,
Please God, forget me not.

I'm 80 next birthday. I can remember when I'd be about eight years old, the days when my mother used to go to the Guardians. They were so hard with her! She didn't get much. She used to get a food ticket. We had treacle more than anything. No such thing as cereals.

We used to have the oatmeal porridge and she used to put bread in a basin and an Oxo cube and we used to have that for our dinner. She'd get savoury ducks and make a pan of potato hash. We couldn't afford meat.

Coal was fivepence a hundredweight. Many a half hundredweight I've dragged in a wagon, because she couldn't afford a hundredweight.

We had to go to bed early because there was no light and we couldn't afford oil every night. I had to be up at five o'clock of a morning because I had to be with my mother at the mill. My father never worked. He was always in hospital.

Girls in the mill worked from six in the morning until half past five at night. They used to get half an hour for breakfast. I'd have to get about eight or nine jugs of hot water ready for them when they came in for their breakfast. They used to give me fourpence for making it.

I used to run a mile for a halfpenny to get tuppence together to go to the magic lantern of a night-time. It was on a big screen in the mission at the Sunday school.

We used to have treats on lorries. Buns in a paper bag. An orange, an apple. Open lorries they were. It was a day out for us, a trip out. Those were the pleasures we got, but the most was the magic lanterns.

Teenagers weren't allowed the liberties they have today! Oh dear no! There was a spiritual hall in Whit Lane and we could get a cup of tea and a pie for fourpence and we'd have a little dance.

As the years went by I used to find my way to the Prince of Wales. It was fourpence to go in. I was getting older then! Those were the days, but the girls today … they'd never live it! Many a time I couldn't go to school because I'd no clogs and my feet was wet – no money for irons.

My mother used to sometimes say, "Don't be late home from school." When I came home, she'd have a big basket and a white cloth inside it and barm cakes, with a cloth over the top. I'd only be out about half an hour and I'd have sold them all. Four for threepence. They went like wildfire. They was barm cakes in those days."

NELLIE POTTER, *a former pit head worker, would have been delighted to have a barm cake to eat at work.*

I didn't work on the screen. I was on t'top, outside. There wasn't a cover. Nothing. After 1926, they boxed it all in. We were wet through. When it was winter, and they was hard winters, our clothes even got frozen to our backs. It was terrible sometimes. You'd have to go round and empty your tub into the creeper. And that went up, this creeper, and on to the weighing machine.

How did you move this tub?

Push it! Push it with your hands.

What did you wear?

A head shawl a yard square, a man's jacket, a long black skirt and a right long black pinny and long black stockings.

Did you get very dirty?

I didn't because I was outside in the open. Those that was on the belts, the screens, they did, because they was in all the dust. I got very greased up; the ends of my skirt used to trail along and catch on the tub wheel.

How did you get the dirt off your clothes, the grease?

Oh it was a job! Often enough you used to have three skirts, one of them drying if it were bad weather …

Were there any facilities to wash?

Not then.

What did you take to eat?

Anything … bread and jam …

Paul must have relived some poignant events from his own years on the road when he interviewed a young Manchester down-and-out.

It's a question of every man for himself, but you certainly need company. They'd be a lot better off if they could band themselves together. Two or three friends could do a great deal for each other: get themselves off the streets; perhaps petition the local council or their MP, or the Government itself, because they certainly would be entitled to assistance.

When I see chaps sitting around all day, they don't seem to have anything to do, anything to look forward to, no pleasure. Sometimes they read newspapers, but just what do you think about, all day long? I don't know, possibly a brighter future, raising yourself up. I think men have a lot of dreams.

And of course it's only natural to think about where the next meal's coming from and possibly how to keep themselves out of the hands of the law.

How much trouble do you have with the law and what kind of trouble?

It's mainly how not to stop too long in one place. They're not very sympathetic towards you. They seem to take a delight in humiliating you.

When you say staying too long in one place, do you mean sleeping out?

Yes, and not necessarily on a park bench ... in an old shed, a toilet, on a blitz site ...

They move you off a blitz site as well as a park bench then?

Yes, if there's an old workmen's site on the edge of a blitz site, and you're sleeping there, they won't leave you there.

Do they ever threaten to run you in for not having any visible means of support?

Oh yes! In fact, that's the usual threat. They threaten to take you down and charge you, or even kick you out of the town. They say you're filthy, a disgrace, goodness knows what else.

How do you find keeping clean?

Just how do you manage it? I've found it rather difficult at times, but there's open toilets, toilets with public wash basins, and every now and then you get one with hot water running and liquid soap. You make the effort, but still you get people against you. Like the other day in St Mary's Gate in Manchester, I was kicked.

How do you get money to eat?

A number of people have been very good. One or two friends have come into the city and always give me two or three shillings, but I've also worked at odd jobs to earn a few shillings, but I must admit, for about a fortnight after I came into the city, I ate by unorthodox means. I've been up to Smithfield and there's been bruised fruit, fruit that was bad and would normally be thrown away and they'd leave out a box full of it.

Do the chaps there leave the fruit out for you? Do they have this feeling for you?

I think they leave it out for anyone, but I think the people who are down and out are most in their minds. It's not good fruit, it's the sort that would be thrown away or used for pig-swill or something.

You mentioned the police. Have you been picked up?

I was having a rest in St Mary's Gate about three weeks ago at about 5.30 in the morning, and a police officer came along with an ordinary constable and took me to Cannon Street but they didn't charge me with being down and out. They upgraded me, if anything, to first class. That means I was a little better off than when I arrived in the city.

What did they say to you when they found you?

They said I was not allowed to sleep out and that I should move on to another city. At Cannon Street, all they asked for was my name and one or two particulars and then said, "You've been downgraded and thrown out of Stockport but the police here have accepted you and upgraded you, first class, one step up."

What's the term for one step up?

It means I'm more or less the same as I am now – I'm one step up from inferior!

Beswick is a district next to Bradford, Manchester. Paul was born and spent his toddling years in Bradford, so there must have been much to interest him as this Beswick man looked back on his own childhood. Yet even for the young, the spring that turned the cogs was money.

These blokes used to come round with a barrel organ. They'd get all the kids sat down and one of the blokes used to get himself up as Charlie Chaplin or summat like that. Fraser, he was called. This was down Ashton Old Road, Beswick, just by the railway.

At the corner of the street was Kitty's, the boozer. They used to go in, have a few gills and then, with all the kids sat down, Fraser would start dancing and singing and all the kids joined in with the songs as was on the organ, popular at the time. They had a lad called Dido with them, who went round the doors collecting, with a box.

Another bloke used to come round with a little organ on a stick and a long pole with a monkey. And it used to climb up on to the roof and if it found a ball up there in the gutter, it would throw the ball down to him. He'd say, "Oh, it's a good ball this. Who'll give me a halfpenny for it, a farthing?" Even a farthing was a lot of money then, for a kid.

Sometimes, he'd get nobody paying up, no halfpennies, like. So we used to get a piece of rope and two of us would go running down the street, one on either side of him. And him, barrel organ and monkey, would go over, all upset in the gutter. And we got the ball like that! If he should catch hold of you, you'd get your arse belted. Booted, never mind belted! And if your old man heard about it, you'd get another leathering.

You could knock a bottle off at Kitty's at the corner. Over the backyard, two bottles, penny each, take them back. And I'd think, well, tuppence, right, two Woodbines, matches, pictures. One of us would dive in. The piss stone was just as you walked in. Ticket out through the window and another one would dive in. So you got two in the pictures, two Woodbines and matches, all for two bottles out of the boozer back.

Course if you got copped, you had to pay for it, Not in money – you paid in kind! My arse has been pummelled scores and scores of times. Kicked. Belted. We used to have some bloody sport then!

Did you know a picture house in Beswick called the Don? The Don pictures, aye. Corner of Mitchell Street and Old Town, Ashton Old Road. We used to go there Saturday afternoon, if you'd got a penny. Get a comic such as *Funny Wonder* or *Chips*, or perhaps you'd get some toffees, an apple or orange, when you was going in. A good penn'orth. Coming out you got a pass. And the following week you could go in with a halfpenny and your pass.

You could go in the Don or the Palmy or the Mosley, using that pass. And if you'd no halfpenny, us being brave, we used to go looking for the littler kids. "Have you got your pass? Well give it here or I'll belt you one!" And when you'd got your pass, you could generally cop for a halfpenny. Then you could get in the pictures.

If you went in the Palmy you got a pass coming out. Palmy, bottom of Palmerston Street. Old woman owned that, she'd be about 60, had a chip shop opposite, and you could change your pass for a paper full of chips. So you got in the pictures and a paper full of chips for a halfpenny.

There was another old woman next door to her shop – Old Mother Waites, the fortune teller. Her lad Jimmy used to knock about with us. She used to sit in a chair with her feet up over the oven. She used to read the tea leaves and she used to get the money, tuppence or threepence and put it in a tin cup in the oven.

This day, we goes in for the cup. We got the oven door a bit open and young Jimmy gets his hand in the cup. It's red hot! He lets out a yell. She's up, over on her back, fell over the cat, and she had a shade in the middle with crystals, you know, a chandelier, big glass shade. Down comes the shade, me on the floor with the shade.

She cops for Jimmy, gives him a whaling then tells my old feller, so I got a whaling.

There was one fellow, Fish Charlie we called him, used to come along the street, and one of the kids had a little dog and the fellow boots this dog and he'd no right to do that. There was no way we could say anything 'cos he'd give us a leathering,

He always stopped near one house. John Dunbar lived there and we decided to get all the cats we could and take 'em upstairs in his back bedroom because he lived with his grandmother and grandfather, they were about 80 and they all slept downstairs. They never went upstairs.

By the end of the week, oh, we must have had a hundred cats upstairs. Saturday dinnertime, Fish Charlie comes, stops outside, starts shouting "Cod alive-o!" and all this caper. We takes the dog in, takes it up the stairs, throws it in the bedroom. Down come all the cats, all over the place, over the fish cart.

Best of it was, John's grandfather always used to sit on a chair near the door. They went over him and you can imagine, there was blood everywhere. Those cats, they was everywhere, they cleared the table, cleared the sideboard, all the vases. That was another one we had to pay for with us arses. We got in some right scrapes.

POACHERS SUCH as **George Hale,** interviewed in 1960, do not risk prison, or the gamekeeper's gun, for the fun of it. They need to sell their catch to pay rent, or to buy food for a hungry family. So money is again the motive force, but even here there is room for a little raw humour.

Then you come up behind the hedge backing and you pull your net out and he gets hold of that end and you get hold of this end and you walk up the field in line.

Now mind, it's dark. But as you're going along, all of a sudden you'll hear a flutter, because your dragging net touches them. They'll flutter up. Then you just let your net drop and you catch 'em and kill 'em. And Bob's your uncle …

We had about six pigs. Some were farrowin'. That were a good time. Then they told us they wanted the flamin' land! And there's never been a bloody thing on it since.

You know Brooklands Road, them little lodges on the

front of it? I was told there was gates on there at one time. It was a private road. There was gates on both sides to stop anybody going in. They had to pay a toll. I've made many a bloody pound on it! Me and Sam used to go down on a Sunday morning when we were stuck for money, when we were about 13 or 14 and we used to mind the gates, while they was having a meal and a snooze.

Anyone as lived on the road could go down. Anyone else, a stranger, they had to pay a shilling. A tanner for motorbikes, but there wasn't many of them. Pushbikes was alright. Not many motor cars. They used to go down there … there were knockin' shops, you know. High class. Anyway, they used to go down and sometimes they'd give you a shilling, even a couple of shilling.

Who was the first you can remember having the Stonemason's?

That would be Atherton.

How long ago was that?

Oh … a long time ago. He must have died. Anyway, they buried him on spec!

Later, on the subject of rabbits …

You put your net at the side of the field. You've got to have the wind coming towards you. You don't want it blowing away from you, up the field. They'll scent you and they'll just go.

When you've staked your net out, you send your dog up to the top of the field and when he gets there, he keeps running back and to, zigzagging, until he comes to you. And he's brought the rabbits down to you and your net.

When they hit the net, some of 'em squark. They make a din, some of 'em. Before they squark too much, you hit 'em on t' back o' neck. Or on t' side. Please yourself. And if you don't get nicked you go to another field …

Once, just the other side of Nob Hall, we'd just got set. The dog had gone out and he were nearly up to the top o' t' field. We were in moonlight. When the moon's out, you get down, and you always keep by the hedge backing. You can see anybody coming in the moonlight. Never cross a field when you're going poaching in moonlight, 'cos they can see you.

Anyway, this night the dog had been out a couple of minutes or so and Jock shakes the net, and pulls it and I knew that he wanted to get the net up, so we start whippin' pegs up quick. Then as we were crossing that stile path over the cart road, a bloody gun went off.

He must have been following us. It was Roger Clark the gamekeeper. The reason he was after us, though he knew it wasn't us, was that in Wythenshawe Park, there was a lot of rabbits and a lot of poachers from Stockport.

Keeper went out once and he must have collared them and they bopped him, give him a bloody good hidin' and by crikey, he died a short while after. And that's why they was always after you.

Going to work in the morning, we used to pick the snares up and once we caught a bloody great big Persian cat in a snare. It was a sort of slate colour. Jock fetched it in and I said get rid of that! Shove it in the fire hole or something. So he shoved it on the boiler hole and burned it. Two days after, Harry Burgess comes up and he said, Hey, did you know? There's a pound reward for a big Persian cat. Jock says, "Oh Christ! We've thrown a pound away there!" He'd have got more than a bloody pound if they'd found out. It had the snare mark round its neck.

Finally, back to Billy Findlow and another terrifying way to earn some much-needed money …

What about tupping?

"That was another sport. That was up on the Dingle too."

The blokes who did the purring, did the same blokes do the tupping?

"One or two, but a lot of blokes from different places: Clayton, Gorton, Ancoats.

Generally, if you got a beer house champ, he was supposed to be able to kick them, and be able to nut them as well. But sometimes, if he wasn't so clever on that, he'd go sick that weekend and they'd put a substitute in.

Our old feller was the tupper for the Cricketer's. That was another where you stood face to face, hands on shoulders, watched the ref and when the cap or the hanky dropped, you went in with your head. You'd try to stick it on him and he'd try to stick it on you and when you went down or you let go, you were finished. If you had a good hard head, a good solid lump of bone up front, you was a good tupper. You didn't want no brain. If you could just go in and start nodding hard and fast, you didn't do so bad.

Some would hold their face up for you and as soon as you went in to hit 'em between the eyes with your forehead, they'd drop their head and you'd hit a lump of bone and many a time, you'd go down.

They nearly all finished with bad eyes, cut eyes. I think round Bradford, Beswick, Clayton, there's more bad eyesight among the old blokes, through tupping, than anywhere in the country.

I've seen them when they were out of work, on the

256

corner, nowt to do and they'd say, "Oh, come on, let's go down the Dingle. Let's have a bit of a knock. I've seen 'em go for nothing. Not purring, but I've seen 'em have a bit of a tupping match. No stakes, just a bunch of blokes with nowt to do.

There was a variation called Knock Apiece. Same rules more or less, but they used to toss up for what they called the first knock. If it was you, the other bloke wouldn't retaliate and you'd set yourself and go in with your head. Whether you hit him or missed him, it was his go, with you stood there. You could move your head to make him miss, if you could. Or if he came in a bit on the slow side and you could drop your head, he could hit himself on the bony part and knock his bloody self out.

It used to go on till one fell on the floor or got knocked out. More often than not, one was knocked out at Knock Apiece. But that was more or less just a pastime sport, when there was nowt to do, no money, perhaps a couple of fags, no money to go in the boozer, so you'd go up the Dingle and pass on an hour or two with that. They used to say there was nowt only solid bone above the shoulders if you worked at the Forge or the pit."

AFTERWORD BY DAVID HALL

That's where we've come from.
Here's where we are.
Where are we going to now?

BEGINNINGS

BY NOW you probably have a picture of Paul Graney as a man both simple and complex. You are not alone. I don't suppose that any of us who have paid our tributes to him ever knew the whole man, but I am certain we all respected, revered and loved him.

Paul's life first touched mine in 1966. At 17, with no family, I was living in a flat in Whalley Range, Manchester. I had been learning the guitar for about ten months and attending folk clubs for about six. Then I was given a banjo. Played with skill, this is the instrument with which Gershwin used to bring tears to strong men's eyes, with his 'Rhapsody in Blue'. I had no skill. I had loudness.

In a neighbouring flat lived an elderly man who wore a beret, smoked a pipe, rose mostly at dawn, walked all over Manchester by day and night, and received parcels from all over the world. One Monday, after a particularly loud practice weekend, we met at the post table and it finally occurred to me to apologise.

The first words ever spoken to me by Paul Graney were: "Play banjo, do you? What sort of music do you like?" And then: "You'd better come and meet my mate. Can you be ready for half past six?" And off he went to work.

That evening he took me and my mate Ken to meet

the Manchester Man himself, the folksinger Harry Boardman, and his wife Lesley.

Harry taught us how to tune and frail a banjo properly and from that night I started to learn what Paul meant by folk music: that it did not have to be on a record; that it did not have to be from America or Ireland; and that there were actually people over 21 who not only liked it but were knowledgeable about it and cared for both the music and the people connected with it.

There were many more like me. People like Mike Harding (teacher), Dave Davidson (youth worker), Packie Byrne (whistle player), the McPeaks (family singers of four generations), Dorothy and Ivan, Tony and Martin, Lorna, several more Mikes, Daves and Petes, Ian, Marie, Ted, Faith, Bob, Thurston … To all these and more, he was 'My Paul Graney'. I don't think Paul was the same to any two people. He had something to give us all.

Later …

Barry Seddon, the editor of this book, has already written about his first meeting with Paul. What he does not say is that on that night I was singing with a folk group. Barry says that Paul listened to us and said, "Aye, they'll do." I still feel a glow of pride … And our performance that night was all thanks to what Paul Graney had given us. Apart, that is, from the meat and tater pie night, and the recipe for a pancake diet. But those are two more long stories.

The Trust …

When Paul died in 1982, suddenly I could not say thank you. Many others must have felt the same. Over his lifetime, Paul had made many hundreds of tape recordings of songs, stories and ordinary people's memories. All anyone had to say was, "I'm interested in such and such" and a few days later he'd hand over a box of tapes: "See if any of this is any good. Let me have it back when you've copied what you want." And in my case, "Oh, haven't you got a tape recorder? Hang on ..." And back he came with my first tape recorder, one of his many gifts.

After the funeral, at which Harry Boardman (now sadly passed on) gave a memorable address, I asked Barry (dreading that he would think me some sort of vulture) what had happened to Paul's collection. "It's safe with me," he said, and I was happy to know that someone else cared and that Barry and his wife Marjorie would not allow Paul's life's-work to die with him. I was surprised and flattered when Barry later suggested that I help him to save the collection, to be used as Paul had, but on a larger scale.

And the Paul Graney Memorial Folk Trust was born. Gifts from industry and individuals and grants from the Association of Greater Manchester Authorities (AGMA), helped us to buy equipment, archive-quality tapes and (eventually) DVDs and computer gear. AGMA also provided a rent-free home at the Greater Manchester County Record Office.

Special nights at folk clubs brought further welcome funding. Then Simon Henniker joined me for the final two years as a paid employee, thanks to a major grant from the Heritage Lottery Fund.

None of Paul's original recordings will be altered. Only second generation copies will be edited, in accordance with good archival practice. Hundreds of copies of a CD called *Work and Play*, all its songs, interviews and photographs, either recorded or taken by Paul, have been given to schools and libraries in Greater Manchester and beyond.

Eventually a formal catalogue will be published and the whole Paul Graney Archive will be available to students, researchers and folk music enthusiasts and – as Paul would have wished – to anyone interested enough.

Meanwhile, this book just might show you another face of that amazing 'One Bloke'.

David A Hall (1949-2008)

How can you get where you're going, if you don't know where you're from?

GLOSSARY

This section, shortened where possible, avoids distracting footnotes. 'Paul' means Paul Graney. The 'Old to New' panel is for those born after decimalisation.

Access To Mountains – Campaign to ensure that ramblers could continue to walk Derbyshire moors and mountains. First Mass Trespass staged at Winnats Pass in April 1932. Jimmy (Ewan MacColl) Miller was there and is believed to have written verses which formed the basis of the rallying anthem, 'Manchester Rambler'. Paul believed they were written in the early 1930s as he, Miller and Joan Littlewood sheltered from the rain in pub.

Agitprop – AGITation + PROPaganda – Spreading of Communist doctrine via films, plays, books, etc. See barnstorming.

Ambler, Jimmy 'Ambler the Rambler' – leading figure in early northern rambling and climbing fraternities.

Armistice Day – 11 November. Anniversary of the armistice that ended the First World War. In 1939, the two-minute silence changed to the Sunday nearest to 11 November, in case the anniversary fell on a weekday, thereby affecting wartime production. After the Second World War, the name changed to *Remembrance Day.* As many now observe silence on 11 November, both Armistice Day and Remembrance Sunday are commemorated formally.

Ballow – see Looms.

BUF – British Union of Fascists, founded by Oswald Mosley in 1932, gained initial support thanks to Mosley's oratory and to backing by *Daily Mail* publisher Viscount Rothermere. People soon recognised the doctrine's nasty roots.

Band club – Brass and silver bands and clubs found in many Northern towns. Nelson no exception. Club would provide band with rehearsal and/or concert room. Costs often met by having public social room – early form of working men's club.

Barnstorming – Touring rural districts to stage plays. Originally, actual barns would be used. American sense of rapid political tour probably closer to agitprop aims of Theatre of Action.

Belting – Heavy leather bands used to drive mill machinery.

Blackshirts – Italian para-military combat groups wore shirts of this colour in violent · opposition to Socialism and Communism. In 1921, became national militia of Mussolini's Fascist party. Hitler's Nazi SS troops also called Blackshirts, term later applied to any Fascist organisation, such as BNP.

Board of Guardians – Local authority body set up to look after people fallen on hard times. Precursor of National Assistance Board. (NAB)

Bog Trotters – According to late Eddie Frow, this was name given to troupe of minstrels/entertainers, usually miners, who toured pubs.

Bolt – Roll of fabric.

Brown, Jackie (1910-1971) – Manchester-born boxer, World flyweight champion from 1932 to 1935. Nicknamed 'Manchester Express' for punching speed. Lost World, European and British titles in Manchester in 1935, at hands of Benny Lynch of Glasgow.

Brownshirts – Hitler's Nazi Storm Troops, founded in 1921, wore shirts of this colour.

Castor oil – Laxative. Mothers used to give children small amount once a week, to keep them 'regular'. In much larger amounts, it was administered as an instrument of discomfort/torture by Mussolini's Fascists.

Closed shop – When every employee of a company must be a union member.

Crabtree, Councillor – When Paul talks of seeing him in *Love On Dole*, he is actually remembering Councillor (later Alderman) Walter W Crabtree (d.1953) appearing in Greenwood's follow-up play, *Give Us This Day*. This was not at Salford Hippodrome, but at Manchester Repertory Theatre, in March 1936. No enemy of the poor, Crabtree preached Socialist propaganda in Hyde Park, led local anti-Fascist battles, was treasurer of the Unemployed Workers' Movement, Salford branch, in the early 1930s and was in several anti-Means Test marches, including one which ended in the Battle of Bexley

Square, Salford, on 1 October 1931.

Croft – Area of open and often derelict land in a town or city.

Dobby – See Looms.

Dole – Contemptuous term for Unemployment Benefit and Relief distributed by NAB or National Assistance Board. Innuendo was that money legally due to jobless people was shameful charity handout to idle spongers.

Dosser's Wedge – Stodgy mixture in its prettied-up 'wine slice' form is well-remembered by my wife. She bought one in the mid-60s only to find it was mouldy – obviously made from cakes that were just *too* old.

Dosshouse – Cheap lodging house where tramp or vagrant could 'get his back down'. French for back is dos.

Duffy – Rough-house fight. Possibly related to phrase 'to duff up'.

Flit – To move house quickly, sometimes by night, often because rent cannot be paid.

Flush – Money to spare. A full purse would have coins flush with its top.

Foulds Mill – There was no Foulds Mill as such in Nelson. 'Room and power' operator named Foulds possibly rented space at Whitefield Shed, part of which was in Maurice Street, where Paul was raised.

Foxglove – Potent heart stimulant digitalis is prepared from dried leaves of this plant. Parents' warnings well-founded.

Gow, Ronald (1897-1993) – Teacher/playwright, born Heaton Moor, near Stockport. Career boosted by successful stage adaptation of Walter Greenwood's *Love on the Dole*.

Greenwood, Walter (1903-1974) – Born Ellor Street, Salford. *Love on the Dole* appeared in 1933 as a novel. Became best-seller in 1934, after Ronald Gow dramatised it for Altrincham Garrick Club. Manchester Rep (also known as Rusholme Rep) took it on tour, starring Wendy Hiller (soon to be Gow's wife). West End success and 1941 film. Before he died in Isle of Man, Greenwood wrote numerous novels, articles, and scripts.

Half timing – Pupils spent half their day in school and the other half in the mill. The practice varied from mill to mill, but was dying out by 1920, particularly in Nelson, where local teachers opposed it.

Hallamshire Harriers – Club formed in 1896 by former members of Sheffield YMCA Harriers, runners and supporters of cross-country and flat running. Sebastian Coe, who broke eight world records, was an outstanding member.

Hallelujah I'm a Bum – American folksong, sung by soldiers during Spanish-American war, by North West loggers and harvest workers and by jobless Americans during 1930s economic crisis. Anthem of jobless when taken up by Wobblies (Industrial Workers of the World).

Hankey Park – Nickname for closely-packed residential district of Salford, now demolished and renamed Broadwalk. Hankinson Way, beside Pendleton shopping precinct, also keeps the name alive. Despite Paul's disparaging words about his play-writing, Walter Greenwood had an eye for vivid detail: 'District takes its name from sloping street, Hankinson Street, whose pavements, much worn and very narrow, have been polished by traffic of boots and clogs of many generations.' When he wrote of its 'tiny houses, cramped and huddled together,' its many public houses and pawnshops, sterile and bleak crofts, all wrapped in a 'constant swirl of blue-grey smoke', he was describing much of the city which inspired Ewan MacColl's 'Dirty Old Town'.

Hobson's Choice – No choice at all – after T Hobson, seventeenth century carrier who hired out horses but whose customers were obliged to take the one nearest the door.

Hunger March – See Jarrow.

Hulme Albion FC – Manchester County Football Association records yield no reference to Paul's teenage team, although Hulme Celtic is mentioned in 1933 as having a ground at Talbot Road, Old Trafford. Paul's team probably did not survive long enough to come to official notice.

Hyndman Hall – Named after Londoner Henry Mayer Hyndman, who founded the Social Democratic Federation in 1884. In 1906, when South Salford branch of SDF outgrew premises on Trafford Road, it acquired 69 Liverpool Street, on the corner of Eliza Street. Paul's top floor gymnasium was a Socialist Sunday school at first, run by Sam Amey and Elsie Farrow. In 1906, the large ground floor club room had a fireplace encircled with the words: 'Workers of the world unite, you have nothing to lose but your chains. You have a world to win.' The hall was demolished in 1974. Liverpool Street Fire Station stands opposite site.

Initiation – Paul's weft cellar ordeal was not as unlikely as some sheltered souls might think. Such ceremonies still happen, ranging from sending apprentices for sky hooks or rubber hammers, to full-blooded ordeals, often sexually embarrassing.

Jarrow March 1936 – Hunger march organised in protest against the Means Test and cruel cuts in the dole. Unique in that it was organised by Jarrow Town Council and involved the whole town.

Jimmy Nelson's – (See Nelson's)

Kitchener – Horatio Herbert, Earl Kitchener of Khartoum (1850-1916). Defeated Dervishes and reconquered Sudan in 1898. Secretary of State for War at start of First World War. Fiery moustaches on posters (Your Country Needs You!) brought forward two million Army volunteers.

Knurl – To make ridges on control knob, making it easier to grip.

Lansbury, George (1859-1940) – Labour MP for Bow and Bromley (1922-1940). On Royal Commission on Poor Laws (1905-1909) and signed famous minority report. During First World War closely associated with pacifist section of Labour Party: powerful defender of conscientious objectors. Helped to set up and later edited Labour's first daily newspaper the *Daily Herald* (1912).

Littlewood, Joan – Working-class girl born 1914, in Stockwell, London; founded eventually world-famous Theatre Workshop, in Stratford. Eightieth birthday autobiography, *Joan's Book* (Methuen 1994) describes Manchester and Salford period when Paul says their paths crossed. Acidly, in letter to me (18 May 1994), said she had not 'faintest recollection' of Paul, adding: 'There were hangers on from time to time.'

Looms – Plains or twills, which Paul mentions, are self-explanatory; dobbies, or patterns, had frame containing pegs in revolving lattices which selected and raised appropriate healds. Checks made by yet another type of loom. Ballow was what I believed Paul was saying each time I listened to his original recording, but I had grave doubts. In August 2009, Carole Hurd, textile gallery presenter at Manchester Museum of Science and Industry, came to my rescue. 'Ballow ends,' she wrote, 'may be local dialect term for mechanism on looms that wove check cloth. Checks were woven on what were called box looms. They had a mechanism on the side which held different coloured shuttles that formed the check pattern. This would turn every time a new colour was inserted. As a rule, it held four different colours. It would turn one way, then would have to be turned back to start again. It was chain-driven and usually barrel-shaped.' *Cotton Manufacturing* by CP Brooks, (Blackburn, 1888 or 1889) is excellent on weaving terminology.

Lord Haw-Haw – Derisory nickname for William Joyce, defector, who broadcast German propaganda to Britain during the Second World War. Hanged as a traitor.

Love On The Dole – See Walter Greenwood.

MacColl, Ewan – See Jimmy Miller

Mangle – Though used for printing, this is clearly a larger version of the old-style domestic wringer, with rollers under pressure. When these were turned, via gear-linked handle, wet washing was pulled through and emerged drier.

Means Test – Introduced in 1931. When someone out of work sought Unemployment Benefit, total family wages were assessed. Young people in work were often made responsible for jobless parents. With no chance of marrying and starting their own families, many therefore left home. Paul's reason for leaving home was different: he was out of work and seeking benefit; mother and sister were working, but unjustly, were being badly treated ...

Miller, Jimmy (1915-1989) – Born in Lower Broughton, Salford, of Scottish parents, both singers. Founded Red Megaphones, agitprop group performing street theatre with crude slogan-shouting as propaganda. Later, with Joan Littlewood, group developed into Theatre of Action. After First World War, Miller (as Ewan MacColl) became well known as a folk singer, with Peggy Seeger.

Model Lodging House – This seems sarcastic, considering conditions in many aptly-named dosshouses. It was in fact an official term, which can be seen moulded into the brickwork of a well-preserved building in Bloom Street, near Salford Station.

Mosley, Oswald – Sir Oswald Ernald Mosley (1896-1980) born in London into family with long-standing connections with Manchester: Mosley Street named after them and former Sir Oswald was city's last Lord of Manor, selling rights to corporation in 1845. Second Sir Oswald entered Commons as Conservative in 1918 but radical suggestions for curing jobless crisis found no favour; joined Labour (1926), attained Cabinet rank under Ramsey MacDonald (1929) but expelled from party in 1931 after radical policies rejected. Established New Party, disbanded it after electoral disaster and founded British Union of Fascists in 1932.

Battle of Cable Street when Mosley took Blackshirts through poor Jewish quarter of East London, led to 1936 Public Order Act banning political uniforms. In 1940, Mosley (friend of Hitler and Mussolini) and second wife, former Diana Mitford, detained in prison as security risks. Mosley died after war at his Paris chateau.

NAB – National Assistance Board. Frequently dealt harshly with unemployed applicants for assistance. Unemployed Workers Movement representatives studied regulations and gained respect when they won some cases. (See Board of Guardians).

Napoleonic Beacons – When Nelson won battle of Trafalgar on 21 October 1805, news was flashed across land by fires on chain of high points such as Pendle Hill.

Nelson's Mill – James Nelson and Son was powerful textile company with 3,700 looms and 320,000 spindles. Had 60,000 spindles in Nelson and owned biggest textile mill there, now demolished.

Nicolson, Harold – Sir Harold George Nicolson (1886-1968). Politically radical diplomat and author. Tried to enter politics in 1931 as member of Mosley's New Party. Failed, but continued to edit party's weekly journal, *Action*. Broke with party in 1932 when it became British Union of Fascists. National Labour MP 1939-1945 and strong supporter of Churchill.

Nutter, Alice – See Roughlee Hall.

NUWM – See Unemployed Workers' Movement.

On tick – On credit. Some shopkeepers allowed regular customers to pay in instalments, each payment ticked off in book.

Panel – When National Health Service began, this word described group of doctors registered in district to accept patients under National Insurance Act.

Peach, L du Garde – Playwright who wrote scripts for Co-operative festivals and rallies.

Pendle witches – See Roughlee Hall.

Powderhall – Edinburgh greyhound stadium. Staged Powderhall Sprint, New Year's Day professional running event, from 1870 until 1971, then transferred to Meadowbank, city's Commonwealth stadium.

Ragwort – Correspondent in Barley, not far from Nelson, says area still 'full of ragwort'. Manchester horticultural expert says that Paul is essentially correct.

Roughlee Hall – Paul is wrong. Hall was empty for a time, but never in ruins. Pendle 'witch' Alice Nutter never lived at Roughlee. It is a popular myth.

Salford Hippodrome – Also known as Windsor, Salford Royal Hippodrome opened in 1904. Demolished in Hanky Park slum clearance (1962).

Skip – Basketwork storage container, often with leather-hinged lid.

Spike – 1. Described in song 'Tuppence on the Rope' as being anchor for one end of rope, over which workhouse transient could drape arms for cheap night's rest;

2. pointed tool used for picking oakum as payment for lodging. This taking apart of old rope produced fibre used in ship caulking.

Strachey, John, (1898-1925) – Editor of *Spectator*. Active unionist free-trader. Opposed state Socialism as contrary to freedom of contract and exchange.

Thous – Thousandths of an inch. Engineering measurement.

Toole, Alderman Joe (1887-1945) – Lord Mayor of Manchester (1936-37).

Unemployed Workers' Movement – Formed as national body in 1921 under leadership of Wal Hannington. Branches organised throughout the country, training members to represent jobless at Courts of Appeal and Boards of Assessors. Local and national Hunger Marches organised, and deputations met unemployment and relief authorities. Salford NUWM branch (see Crabtree) led 1931 fight against Means Test and drastic reductions in unemployment benefit from 18 shillings to 15 shillings and threepence. This led to Battle of Bexley Square [*Salford*] on 1 October 1931, the week before Manchester marchers ambushed.

Uncle's – Euphemism for pawn shop.

Warp – See weft.

Weft – Thread which is woven backwards and forwards, under and over warp threads on loom, to make various fabrics, from tape to bed sheets.

Wragge, Lemuel – Anonymous letter to *Manchester Evening News*: 'Lemuel Wragge was plausible character. I remember sending him a Christmas card when he was in Strangeways Prison for bigamy and also him coming to see if we had survived the great storm on June 18, 1930. I have been in farming all my life but I have not heard of Knob End farm. It was Herod farm. When Lem first came to it he wore riding breeches and leggings and carried a 12-bore shotgun. Old Charlie Knott, who worked for my father, wished him Happy New Year and Lem gave him five shillings. Charlie afterwards said: "That's the sort of man that should have money!"'

OLD MONEY TO NEW

All change! Decimalisation was on 15 February 1971. With the $\frac{1}{2}$p long gone, it is now nearly impossible to convert small amounts from old to new. Approximations follow…

Pre-decimal	Amount	Present decimal
Halfpenny	$\frac{1}{2}$d	1p
Penny	1d	1p
Three ha'pence	$1\frac{1}{2}$d	1p
Tuppence	2d	2p
Tuppence ha'penny	$2\frac{1}{2}$d	2p
Threepence	3d	2p
Threepence ha'penny	$3\frac{1}{2}$d	2p
Fourpence	4d	3p
Fourpence ha'penny	$4\frac{1}{2}$d	3p
Fivepence	5d	3p
Fivepence ha'penny	$5\frac{1}{2}$d	3p
Sixpence (tanner)	6d	3p
Shilling (bob)	1/-	5p
One and six	1/6	8p
Florin (two bob)	2/-	10p
Half crown (two and six)	2/6	13p

Former journalist Barry Seddon, eldest of a hairdresser and a plasterer's five children, was born in Swinton, near Manchester in 1938. A Founder Scholar at Manchester Grammar School, he started in 1955 as a reporter on the weekly *Swinton and Pendlebury Journal*. He married in 1957, and he and his wife Marjorie have two children and two grandchildren

After National Service in the RAF, Barry became a sub-editor on the *Daily Telegraph* in Manchester, before moving to the *Manchester Evening News*, rising eventually to be an Assistant Chief Sub-Editor. He was a staunch union member and member of the NUJ chapel committee. He was at the *News* for 23 years, with casual shifts on most of the Manchester-based daily and Sunday papers.

For five years, he wrote the *MEN's* first folk music column and became a friend of Paul Graney, the region's premier folklore expert. The Memory Tapes which Paul left in Barry's care, form the basis of this book.